Mary Jane Adams

The Choir Visible

Vol. 1

Mary Jane Adams

The Choir Visible
Vol. 1

ISBN/EAN: 9783337296391

Printed in Europe, USA, Canada, Australia, Japan

Cover: Foto ©Thomas Meinert / pixelio.de

More available books at **www.hansebooks.com**

The Choir Visible

by Mary M. Adams

Published by
Way & Williams
CHICAGO

Mdcccxcvii

TO

C. K. A.

CONTENTS

ODES
The Choir Visible	Page 11
Ode to Poetry	15
Lincoln at Gettysburg	39
The Violet	45
The Blush Rose	49
A Song of Springtime	51
Commencement Ode	52
Hymn to Wisdom	64
Invocatory Ode	67
Wedding Hymn	70
Memorial Day	74
Salutamus	81

LYRICS
Redeeming Love	82
Prayer	83
Trust	84
Communion	85
Worthy Thy Gospel	86

Hymn for Forefathers' Day	Page 87
Dedication Hymn	89
Easter Hymn	91
Thanksgiving	92
Light at Eventide	95
Communion with Christ	96
Child's Hymn	97
Love and Work	98
Mizpah	99
The Christmas Gift	100
Gethsemane	101
Scars	102
There is a Star	103
Funeral Hymn	104
The Bird in the Belfry	106
The Bard's Epitaph	107
Dead Love	109
Russia	110
Songs without Words	111
The Bird at Midnight	112
Cradle Song	114
Earth's Requital	116
Labor's Gift	117
Serenity	118
The New Year	119

The Poet's Gift	Page 120
My Best Poem	121

SONNETS

Man and Nature	125
Dawn	128
To Cynthia	130
To the Old Year	131
Winter	134
Easter	136
Easter Morning in the Mountains	137
St. Andrew's Eve	138
To G. H. E.	139
To the Trees on my Lawn	140
To an Anemone	142
Evening on Lake Monona	143
Mount Desert	144
To Shakespeare's Mother	145
The Seraph's Song	146
Hamlet	147
Antigone	148
Dante	149
Birthday of Burns	150
Wordsworth	151
Keats	152

Oliver Wendell Holmes	Page 153
Washington	154
Lincoln	155
Lucius Fairchild	156
Horace Howard Furness	157
One "whose Price is above Rubies"	158
To a Mother	159
To a Friend	160
To the Author of "Songs of Night and Day"	161
To a Beautiful Child	162
The Promise	163
To the Teacher on his Birthday	164
The Educator	165
Baccalaureate Sunday	166
Emperor and Martyr	167
Washington's Birthday	168
Armenia	169
The Artist	170
The Faithful Servant	171
A Golden Wedding	172
Love's Youth	173
Love's Power	174
Where Love is there is Harmony	175
To the Madonna	176

Forgiveness	Page 178
God's Face Reflected	179
The Sabbath Type	180
Poetry of Lincoln	181
Light	182
On the Opening of a New Library	183
On the Opening of a Memorial Guild Hall	184
Love's Gift	185

THE CHOIR VISIBLE

THE choir invisible we praise;
    But I would join the choir I see,
    Of noble souls, who, glad and free,
The living of the world upraise.

Who live to foster all that's right,
    To quicken all that's great and high,
    Yet listen to the feeblest cry,
And strive to make earth's darkness bright.

Who feel the stir of kinship true
    With all who suffer, all who live;
    And who to every creature give
The right to every creature due.

Who breathe a sympathetic song,
    And live the love of One of old
    Who gathered sinners to his fold,
And taught that only sin was wrong.

Who stand wherever Duty calls,
    Nor faint nor falter at her voice,
    But in its least command rejoice,
And feel her blessing ere it falls.

Who bear the burden of the day,
    And know it not, and ask not why
    The neighbor standing idly by
Shall seem to hinder all the way.

Who, though themselves be judged, judge not,
    Nor see in brother's eye the mote;
    But all that is of worth denote,
That good may be of good begot.

Yet from the evil good distil;
    And so, transforming loss to gain,
    The only life of loss retain,
Its single law of life fulfil.

Who never utter thought unkind,
    Nor speak the word reflecting blame;
    And though they know another's shame,
Love's all-concealing mantle find.

Who swell the harmony of life,
    And lessen all discordant tone,
    Their hearts responsive to the moan
Of those who suffer in the strife.

Who with the largest bounty give
    That which in good all else exceeds,
    And, giving self, inspire the deeds
That prove man's highest claim to live.

Who, though they know defeat, stand fast,
    Secure and strong, without alarm,
    Serenely conscious that no harm
O'ertakes the line at anchor cast.

And know that Nature, as in days
    Of Calvary and Gethsemane,
    Keeps still a deep-toned melody,
And chants it in such victor's praise.

Who hate the false, who love the true,
    And live the truth at any cost;
    And though the life be counted lost,
Know well the touch that can renew.

O noble souls! I feel your power,
    You gladden all my earthly way;
    You change its night to joyful day,
You gild the clouds that darkest lower.

With you is life eternal now;
    No loss can touch what you bestow;
    And though the form be mouldering low,
The spirit can itself endow

With changeless form that never dies,
    Nor yet returns unto its source;
    But grows from man to man, a force
That lives by what itself supplies.

Oh, may your blessing on me fall;
    So sway my mind, my heart, my soul,
    That I unto the Perfect Whole
May answer when its music call.

Thus may I join the choir I see;
    Thus add to earth's immortal song;
    Its highest, noblest note prolong,
Till life share all its harmony.

Then will my Heaven begin while here,
    And life reflect from whence it came;
    And love, by its recording flame,
Make all its own great meaning clear.

ODE TO POETRY

I

GOD spake and said, Let there be light;
With bridal blush East kissed the Morn;
God smiled, beholding scene so bright:
That moment Poetry was born.

II

O Smile of God, grant me one ray
    To weave into my lay!
All idle shall its dearest tribute be,
Unless it have inspiring light from thee.

    Come with thy great majesty,
    With passion-crowned tranquillity,
    With thy true sublimity,
    With thy perfect sympathy;
Give of thyself some part to me,
    While I sing of thee;
In thy splendor come, with glory rife,
And let me taste the joy of thine eternal life!

    If I sing not in empyreal rays,
        Of what avail my praise?
    And if thy radiance prove too great,
        Oh, fear not, nor abate

Thy gift: if with thee I fly,
I shall be content to die,
For, sitting on Olympus height, like Semele,
'T will be revealed to me
However dull the human clod,
If ruled by thee, it may become a god.

Come, oh, come with thy celestial power,
And guide my vision for a single hour;
Yet if thou withhold, still must I sing,
And to thy mighty pinions cling,
Trusting to catch some answering gleam
In the very grandeur of my theme.

III
See, she cometh through the eastern gate,
    With heart elate,
      Even as on the morn
        When she was born;
The witchery of unending youth,
The radiance of unfaltering truth,
    Shining on the place
    Where she has turned her face,
    With its freshness and its grace;
And where she treads, all melodies abound,
    For it is holy ground.

                Like the morning,
All beautiful is her adorning ;
                By night, by day,
                She glorifies the way ;
                On land and sea,
                By tide or lea ;
But ever must her surest splendor be
        In the gift she brings to thee,
        To thee, O nation and O man ;
        For brief must be thy span,
If in thy heart she have no place,
        And upon thy life no trace ;
For where no vision is, or seer,
The people perish and the night is near.

                        IV

Behold her as she walks with flowers,
And through the year a June embowers ;
        List, her step upon the field,
Where barren places beauty yield ;
Find her in the forest glade,
Voiceful by her whispers made ;
Hear her in the rippling brook,
        In its foliage-covered nook,

Fit spot for lovers' promise-laden vows,
Whose hope her touch with life endows.

Hearken to her laughter in the waves,
Her deeper cadence in the rock-bound caves;
See the illimitable loveliness of snow
Whereon her footsteps come and go;
Find her in the silence, whose majestic speech,
All wordless, will life's deepest wisdom teach;
Watch her throned upon the breast of Night,
    Its sovereign her satellite,
As all the mighty hosts grow bright
Quiring her joy, while the clouds she presses
And woos them with her soft caresses.
Brighter than the sunbeam at high noon,
Fairer than the ray of fairest moon,
    Is her kiss on each and all,
    And the glory she lets fall.
    Wherever Nature lives,
    She reigns and gives
Her song, her life, her love,
With the joy that cometh from above;
And on the impress of its day
Breathes the life that fadeth not away.
But ever must the surest splendor be
    In the gift she brings to thee,

To thee, O nation and O man;
    For brief must be thy span,
If in thy heart she have no place,
    And upon thy life no trace;
For where no vision is, or seer,
The people perish and the night is near.

V

As from nuptial kiss she came,
    Ever in her name
Shall Love receive his dearest fame.
Through her his wisdom is allied
    To all that life has deified;
    Highest, noblest, fairest, best,
    Royally to him addrest;
Yet hear her say, 'Not unto me,
    O Love, not unto me,
    But unto thee
Shall the praise and glory be;
I am the Smile, thou the Heart of Deity.'
Love answers, 'I am incomplete
Until mine eyes thy radiance meet.
Thy hand alone my crown prepares,
Thy service all my glory shares.
I sometimes know the sight of sin;

With thee its foulness cannot enter in.
I see in life the good, but know the ill.
Thou dost interpret unto me the everlasting will ;
    Convey to me that happiness
Is owning God and nothing less.'

    Listen now
Where souls respond to marriage vow ;
    What bliss she lends,
No other e'er such blessing sends ;
Even here she bids us see
The hope of her eternity.
Through sunshine and through cloud,
    We hear her message loud ;
That witness still shall testify
    To the life that does not die.
In the light of her sweet being,
Happy hearts their Eden seeing,
    Find the paradise within,
Without the tempter and the sin.

    With her all desolation
    Finds an answering salvation
In trust that sees beyond the strife,
The glow of one unending life.

She gives to faith its coronal,
To loyal souls their festival.
And when she leads across the sea,
To shining heights men call paternity,
    With jewel she endows
    Each new Madonna's brows,
Immortal radiance all its ray begetting,
Immortal light forever in its setting.
    Love has then his holiday,
And in the winter keeps the heart of May.

O Smile of God, deign thou with us to dwell
Until all love thy loftiest light compel!
Give unto our hearts its place ;
Leave upon our lives its trace ;
For ever must the surest splendor be
In the gift life gains from thee ;
For where no vision is or seer,
The people perish and the night is near.

VI

    Holier works appear ;
    Grander melodies we hear!
With them the hills of God we climb,
And learn their harmonies sublime,

Uttered by those upon whose lips she laid
The ruddy kiss that cannot fade;
Who looked within her heart and saw
The secret of her heaven-appointed law;
    Made it their own,
    Until upon their labor shone
' The light that never was on land or sea,'
Revealing to the soul its own immensity.
How quickening is its smallest beam!
How nobly men have toiled to gain its gleam!
Gaining, they have scaled eternal height,
And brought to earth the greatness of their flight
With cherubim and seraphim allied,
Henceforth the ills of earth defied,
    Clarifying all life's history,
    Beautifying all its mystery,
    Proving self-subduing victory
    Can banish ill,
    And the world with wisdom fill;
    Gazing inward, still can find
    The best in Nature's mind
And man's; can hear the throb of heartstrings
In the pulsing of the ages; on her wings
Speeding backward, learn of her to free,
Yea, exalt each sense, and be
    Exponent of life's destiny.

Supplying unto souls that thirst
The wine of God ; showing raiment that shall first
Enfold His flesh.   Leading men to see
   Himself in our humanity.

   O Man Eternal,
Owning now her gift supernal,
Rise, and do not doubt,
   But of thyself give out !
Let thy labor show thy thought,
And all that thou hast wrought,
   In silence or in crowd ;
   Be no more unsought ;
   Its gift allowed,
   Let men in homage speak,
   And, strong or weak,
   Award the victor's wreath,
   Nor let its thorns annoy,
But prove in later day and men
The nobler heroes and the greater Troy.

   Let thy voice in noblest lay
      Be the singer of to-day.
   Herald all its glories forth,
   Until men shall see its worth ;

      Use it as becomes its light,
    Increase its witness for the right,
      Make its gift of prophecy
        Banish every falsity,
Sending on to re-create the new,
The good, the beautiful, the true.
      Make thou another marriage feast,
      Invite the greatest and the least,
There transubstantiate to gain
      Life's load of pain;
    Turn the water into wine
      By glance divine,
'Till those who drink in spirit bow
And say, ' The best is with us now.'

      Poet, deign
    To rule and reign.
For ever must the surest splendor be
    In the gift we win from thee;
And where no vision is, or seer,
The people perish and the night is near.

VII

Find her once again within the symbols,
　　Where hearts seek
　　The eternal hope to speak,
　　Varying from year to year,
　　Yet ever keeping pathway clear
　　To the realm from whence she came,
　　Where to-day as yesterday the same
　　　Uplifting strength remains,
　　　And longing soul attains
The mount where God's own ' Very good '
　　Is completely understood.
Where kiss upon His vesture laid,
Abides His time and is repaid;
Endurance in the royal heart begun,
Triumph by celestial patience won ;
　　　This she opens to our view,
Lights the way and leads us through.

　　　Ideals in her hand
Become the real for which they stand,
　　Point beyond and typify
　　Unchanging thought for man
　　　In the great Creator's plan,

Show how he labors on to consummate
    Each hope — perpetuate
His love, longing still to see
Man's soul with his in perfect harmony.
And no exclusive law has she
    Limiting man's sanctity;
    For the lowliest and the least
She shows the temple and the great High Priest.

Would you find the glory in the cloud,
Before which all the stars have bowed?
Gain through her the inner sight,
And, bathed in its auroral light,
    The Hidden Face will be revealed
And all that was before concealed.
Truth, not then without us, but within,
Safe beyond the babble and the din,
    Our every hope surprises
In the blessedness wherein it rises;
    Mercy takes the place of fears;
A rainbow now across the years
    Illumes the mystery of tears.
    While the spirit's ardor burns,
    Nor lowliest aspiration spurns;
    Finding Highest in creation,

Feeding human inspiration,
Raising oft the veil between
Our mortal eyes and the Unseen.
With her the handmaid Duty
  Is transformed to Beauty;
    True renunciation
  Finds the largest consecration,
And we learn that life, not creed,
  Is the universal need.
The humblest then, as worker, priest, or seer,
Walks with his Lord and knows no fear.

        Thus does earth
Obtain the secret of immortal birth,
    And writes upon its record still
That good finds tomb for every ill.

O Smile of God, come with thy quickening ray;
  Show the God-head in the clay;
To every heart the poet's favor bring;
    Let swelling chorus sing, —
      'The vision now is here,
      The symbol's meaning clear;
      No longer ruled by fear,
    Shade and shadow disappear.'

VII

Thou day-beam from on high,
To us this hour draw nigh;
Smile and symbol still of Deity,
Come and answer thou our plea
For the deeper life in thee.

Our need is great;
Our hope returneth desolate;
We see men's hearts in grovelling way,
　　Recognizing not the day;
　　Breathing, but not living,
　　Getting, but not giving;
　　Brazen in an age of gold,
　　Its heavenly alchemy untold;
　　Yearning not, but leading
To the lowest tempter's pleading;
　　Deaf to brothers' cry and call,
　　Dead to sisters' agony;
Waiting beast-like in the stall
　　Of their own up-building;
　　Wrong and error gilding,
　　Sin's progency increasing,
While the hour its sorrow leasing

Passes on, and inharmonious madness
Adds itself to earth's unmeasured sadness.
Thy presence fair is everywhere,
    All thy beauty fills the air;
But the blind eye knows no sight,
Though a universe of suns give light.
    The deaf ear hears no prayer,
    Whatever saint its words prepare.
Breathe thou upon the ear that's sealed
    Until a great Belief hath healed;
    Touch thou the eye that's blind,
And bid its night thy witness find;
Break the captive's fetters, and set free
The soul all mindless of its own vacuity.
    To thy habitations lead
    And on living waters feed.
Let all our deeds be by thy radiance crowned,
Our thoughts in semblance of thyself abound;
    Charity thy wisdom know,
    Passion with thy purity o'erflow,
    All unsoiled its virtue keep
And in thy hands its highest purpose reap.
    Let Laughter, daughter of the sun,
    Fill the world with happier glee,
Drinking deep from fountains of Felicity.

Imagination own,
  Make there thy throne;
  Rule thou our faith,
Its every portion consecrate,
Its hope to deed translate,
Dedicate it through thy grace,
From it all impurity efface;
Let its exaltation be
To reach the heart of God, and see
How infinite is Love's capacity.

No more then shall it sleep or slumber,
But, like the mountain-echoing thunder,
Reverberate with music from on high,
The discord of the world defy,
Changing all earth's deep affliction
  To unchanging benediction.
  Clothed with immortality,
Yet wearing a divine simplicity,
While Reason gains its loftiest sight
  In its serenely purifying light.
In that rosy dawn where thou wert born,
Steep each sense, until we know the bliss
  Of thine awakening kiss,
  And own the newness of thy morn.

    Then shall we find,
    With hallowed mind,
Every sunrise has thee for its guest,
As true as when the East in silence prest
The Dawn, and folded her upon his breast.
And every day thy beauty doth entrance,
Yea, adorn each smallest circumstance ;
    And every place
Show thee not darkly, but as face to face.
    O Smile from Him,
  Be not in our nature dim ;
  Take possession of our souls ;
  Create the longing that controls.

    Sun descending,
    Night defending,
    Gift to men,
    Come as when
God heard the angelic chorus swell
His own assuring sentence, 'All is well.'
Lift thou our eyes unto the hills,
Until the gaze life's tumult stills ;
In lonely or in crowded way,
    Preserve thy sway ;
Lead us as we view men's thought and deed,

And hear thee plead
For the justice all men need;
Then shall music take the place of moan,
And bloom for barrenness atone.

Come and once again inspire
Living souls to use thy lyre;
Let it sound the newer song,
The older symphony prolong!
Waken to immortal birth
    Sons of earth;
Bid unworthy contest cease,
The hour's imperilled heritage release,
    Glorious in its majesty;
And while striving to make free,
    Exhaustless in nobility,
Yet stifled with a tyranny
As odious in its infamy
As ever darkened human way
And closed the portals to eternal day,
    Bid one espousèd self arise
To keep the pathway open to the skies.
Own thou his heart, then look within to read
And sing the song attuned to human need.

Poet, Prophet, Priest, and Seer,
   Unto every nation dear,
   Come thou to ours
   With transcendent powers.
We need thine all-transfiguring grace
   Across our meadowland of space.
   We need to hear thy voice,
      Bidding us rejoice.
Translate for us the music in the air;
   Interpret all that is most rare.
   In thy plenitude of power,
Help us guard our land's enriching dower,
   Its opulence of greatness sent
   To be a people's instrument,
   And advance God-given plan
To make complete His servant, Man.

   Be the watchman on the height,
      To tell us of the night;
Save us from its danger and its threat;
   Show us where the stars are set.
   Arise and be our Prometheus,
   Who without defrauding Zeus
   Supplies the fire for mortals' use;
   Stand upon the new Caucasus.

    Subdue its vulture, chain and rock,
    And its subtler mysteries unlock.
      Show men the freedom that enslaves;
      Point to the liberty that saves.
    Hold the sword with awful flaming,
    And the jewel with the heavenly naming.
    Be the word made flesh; dwell
      Among us, and thy gospel tell.
For ever must the surest splendor be
    In the gift we gain from thee;
And where no vision is or seer,
The people perish and the night is near.

VIII

      To-day, to-day,
  O Smile of God, to-day,
Add thy light unto our lay;
Come with heaven-illuming rays,
Show thyself within our praise.
    Enter now our temple gate,
Be our gracious guest of state,
    While with royal homage meet
We lay our offering at thy feet.

Come, Music, with celestial gift,
In her praise thine anthems lift;
Come, Song, with thy diviner ring,
All her long-earned tribute sing;
Come, Color, and let canvas speak,
Where words shall idle seem or weak;
Come, Marble, and again embrace
Her beauty, and its features trace;
Come, Art, and prove thyself divine,
Because her glories in thee shine.
Come all things that are good and rare,
Make her thine handmaid and her trophies wear.
Ye hillsides, laugh in answer to her glance;
Ye mountains, robe her, and your lights enhance;
Ye meadows, bring to her your sheaves;
Ye trees, exult to show her in your leaves;
Ye valleys, in your dimplement reveal
Her kiss, that ye in loving ardor steal;
Ye brooks, laugh on to see her at your side;
Ye seas and rivers, bring her on each tide;
Ye flowers, enwreathe for her your crown;
Ye grasses, waving, whisper her renown;
Ye cataracts, enfold her as ye leap;
Ye precipices, build her altars steep;
Ye moon and stars, beam on her as ye shine;
Ye greater lights, proclaim her melodies divine;

All that has life in one enraptured psalm
Her greatness and her gifts embalm.
Yet most triumphant shall her honors be
When, O Man, she gives herself to thee.
Then holy, holy, holy, is the song on high,
And holy, holy, holy, does the world reply.
Come, then, O Goddess of the light,
Bring in thy reign without one starless night!
   Bring thy vision of the sun,
   As when thy loveliness was won.
Bring again the vernal sweetness
That enfolds thine own completeness;
Awake one utterance impassioned,
Showing how thy praise is fashioned.
   Kindle in us those undying fires
   That light imperishable desires.
Effulgent keep the life between
Our souls and all that is unseen.

But see, she comes! away all fleeting doubt, away!
   She is with us here to-day.
Behold, in coronation robe she stands
To receive the tribute of thy hands.
   Sound, sound, one rapturous song!
   Over the land its strain prolong.

Away, all fleeting doubt, away!
    She is with us here to-day;
Our hearts respond unto her sway.
See her smile, as East and West
Place their jewels on her breast.
    See her touch upon the brow
        Of our sunny Southland now.
    Watch her beckon to the North,
        As it brings its treasure forth.
Away, all fleeting doubt, away!
    She is with us here to-day.
Here to show us still the throne
    Builded ever for her own;
Here to teach us how to tell
    Her own unending miracle;
Here to show us how the shade of wrong
Dissolves in one undying song;
Here to tell us how in lowliest things
Some voice seraphic has its whisperings.
Here to swell the melody earth hears,
High above the music of the spheres,
Rising from the soul that feels itself a part
Of every breathing, throbbing heart;
Here to show us what is free
    In Love's divinest ecstasy;

Here to foster, not to-morrow's splendor,
But to-day's light, beautiful and tender.
Here to lead us to the height,
And roll away the shades of night.
Here to speak God's word in accents clear,
    To make His light appear,
To show that where no vision is, or seer,
The people perish and the night is near.

LINCOLN AT GETTYSBURG

A NATION'S voice, a nation's praise,
    About its honored dead;
The spot where on eventful days
    Its heroes fought and bled;
The spot where Freedom's spirit spoke
    In words sublime and true,
And where her trumpet tone awoke
    The old song and the new.

The old song with the newer strain,
    To make the first complete,
With melody that lives attain
    Through victory and defeat!
O sacred spot! thrice sacred now
    As years thy record prove!
Before thy shrines all patriots bow,
    These shrines all doubts remove.

The patriot's heart with ardor glows,
    Remembering proffered lives;
He hears in one strong breeze that blows,
    'Life goes, but Love survives,'

The love that stirs a nation's heart
    And bears a nation's fame,
Wherever brave deeds have a part
    And men such deeds proclaim.

He knows its thrilling music tells
    Of those who fell asleep,
And here found tombs, while muffled bells
    A nation's birthday keep.
He hears as well the tender moan
    That in its cadence sings
For those who sit henceforth alone,
    Whose muffled bell still rings.

He hears the added strain it bears
    For all who bravely fought,
For him who in the silence wears
    The scars the battle brought;
Who wears them with a hero's might,
    And honors still the hour
That won a nation's priceless right,
    And proved a nation's dower.

He hears it when it brings the name
    That won a martyr's crown,
Our glorious chief, whose stainless fame
    His country's best renown.
It brings the matchless words he said,
    Standing above their sod,
In hour whose burning import led
    A people nearer God.

It is not ours to dedicate
    This piece of earth so dear,
Nor is it ours to consecrate
    The deeds men witnessed here;
That has been done by those who died,
    On nation's altar slain;
They have these hillsides sanctified,
    Oh, prove it not in vain!

Great leader true! throughout all time
    The world shall hear thy voice;
Because of thee, a holier chime
    Bids Liberty rejoice.

'T was fitting you should tell of those
    Who wrote in blood their song,
And here thy nobler thought disclose
    How nations shall be strong.

How brave men shall perpetuate
    The freedom bravely won,
Forbid that treason desecrate
    What loyal sires begun;
And here on this great field to-day,
    In memory of thy birth,
Let nation's love its tribute pay,
    And echo round the earth.

But let our tribute reach the height
    Thy larger manhood saw,
That broad humanity, whose light
    Was thy diviner law;
That law whose good is absolute,
    Whose mandate, strong and pure,
From every ill can good transmute
    And make its change secure.

If thus we find our gift in thee,
    Its vaster strength will live
To prove its own integrity
    In what we aim to give;
In sense of duty nobly met,
    In nature nobly plain,
In love of men, sublimely set
    In diadems of pain.

In statesman of heroic mould,
    His country's great high priest,
Whose human heart could still enfold
    All things, the great, the least;
Who proved to earth that simple trust
    Is more than Norman blood,
That who would rule must first be just,
    The great must first be good.

To love is ever to ascend;
    Oh, let our love, like thine,
The nation's highest good attend,
    And with thy spirit shine!

Thus shall our tribute catch from thee
    Its worthiest, noblest, best,
And one united country see
    Thy life's divine bequest.

O Gettysburg! thy living dead
    Speak still across the years,
And by their voice our hearts are led
    Above all passing fears;
But keep, O hills! one record true,
    And one great captain's name;
Oh, then shall all men see in you
    A nation's deathless fame!

THE VIOLET

O VIOLET, sweet violet,
    Within thy tender leaves,
What mystic message speaks to me,
    What hidden story breathes?

Each purpling leaflet seems to strive
    To whisper unto me;
But though I feel thy perfumed breath,
    Thy tale is still with thee.

And still my wondering quest must ask
    What power within thee lies
To waken thoughts 'too deep for tears,'
    Yet thoughts that end in sighs?

What sorrowing spirit gave thee birth?
    For still I seem to feel,
When I inhale thy tender breath,
    Some strangely sad appeal.

Oh, wert thou born in Paradise,
    In that dark, fateful hour
When Eve first heard the tempter's voice,
    And yielded to its power?

Or did'st thou blossom where she stood
    When, full of anguished fears,
She sought forgiveness for her sin,
    And wept repentant tears?

Or did'st thou bloom beneath her feet,
    When, by the angel led,
She looked her last on Paradise,
    And knew its hopes were fled?

Or did the air first feel thy breath
    When one great heart and brave
Died for his Lord?   Did'st thou awake
    To mark his lonely grave?

Perchance thy bloom first saw the light
    When Love wooed love in vain,
And Venus, moaning her sad fate,
    Wept for Adonis slain.

Or do thy leaves reflect the light
    That lives in angels' eyes,
When, looking down from heavenly height,
    They hear weak children's cries?

Or art thou but the breath of one
    Who wore her life away,
Because a sin she deemed too dark
    Forbade her lips to pray ?

Or does the light I find in thee
    Come from the patient smile
Of one who wore a crown of pain,
    Unmurmuring the while ?

Or did'st thou catch the weary sighs
    Wrung from a noble soul,
Compelled to climb another's stair,
    And eat a loveless dole ?

Perchance thou art from those dark tears
    That grief-crowned mothers shed,
When yet they stand with empty arms
    Above their first-born — dead.

And yet — O thought too dear to speak ! —
    If tears brought thee to light,
They surely were the tears of Him
    Who made our darkness bright.

For He alone could give to grief
    A power so strangely sweet,
And He alone could give to woe
    A fragrance so complete.

O lovely flower! how vain my quest!
    Thou wilt not answer me;
The wondrous secret of thy life
    Must still abide with thee.

And wise art thou; thy treasure keep;
    It is enough to know
That thou dost live, that from thy leaves
    Such mystic meanings flow.

But this I pray: if from my tears
    One flower should ever bloom,
Oh, may it speak in breath like thine,
    And yield as sweet perfume.

THE BLUSH ROSE
(Its blush — whence came it?)

LOVE went roaming one summer day;
  Within a garden he chose to stray.

Under a swaying rose-tree near
A maiden slept and knew no fear.

The blossoms above were not more white
Than her fair bosom — naked quite

To Love's rapt gaze; one dimpled arm
Pillowed her head, and the mystic charm

That Innocence knows gave to her face
A beauty greater than Love can trace.

' Love's place is here,' and bending low
He kissed her bosom, white as snow.

A blush, suffusing cheek and brow,
Steals swiftly over the maiden now;

And a feeling never known before
Enters her young heart's inmost core.

Innocence gazes in mute alarm,
And steals away while the blush is warm.

' This blush is mine — not Love's,' she said.
Another moment, and she had fled.

Passing, she touched the roses near;
They felt the power of her sweet fear.

And the blush she carried away that hour
Fell on them with a secret power;

And the buds that oped to the air that night
Were blushing red in the morning light.

A SONG OF SPRINGTIME

THERE is a song a poet sings,
    That to my heart true comfort brings;
It tells in such assuring way
The year's good promise of the May;
And oft amid the winter gloom,
When days are dark, and wanting bloom,
I whisper o'er the glad refrain:
'The spring will soon be here again.'

But catching now its echo sweet,
I breathe it into prayer most meet,
For you, O tender heart and true,
To whom my soul is wed anew;
May each new year your May-time bring,
And, lingering, may its gladness cling,
To brighten all your winter gloom,
When days are dark and wanting bloom,
And bid you hear the glad refrain:
'The spring will soon be here again.'

COMMENCEMENT ODE

I

WHAT noble deed
    Will each one bring
To crown the years, whose echoes ring
Within these halls?
    What clamoring need
    Will each one meet
    As forth he goes with eager feet
Into the world, to falter, fall, or lead?
Oh, let no trifler answer here,
With boastful or with timid cry
    Make his reply!
The hour demands a deeper thought,
A longing with high purpose fraught,
And every worthy lesson caught
    Afar or near.

II

The breast-plate that your Mother gives,
On which her name untarnished lives,
    Will you with stainless virtue wear,
    And her dauntless motto bear,
    Until the day is done
    And for her your trophy won?

Oh, guard it even as your life!
    Let no unworthy strife
        Its brightness dim.
Add to its lustre, if you will,
    The story of your skill,
        Whatever be your fate,
        In lowly place or great,
Give to the days your best,
And leave with God the rest.

III

    This glorious hour
    Is pregnant with undreamed-of power.
      'T is yours to use,
      'T is yours to lose;
    You cannot its gift refuse.
Shall not the Right know truer ring
Because of all your acts shall bring?
Shall not the Truth reveal her own
Because her light within you shone?
Shall not each day your wisdom prove,
Nor power of earth your honor move?
    These questions you alone must meet,
    As forth you go with eager feet.

Oh, answer well!
By life, by thought, by tongue, by pen,
Prove you are men!

IV

The portal swings to darkness wide,
And all your paths are yet untried;
But hope before you runs
With quenchless torch, nor shuns
The darkest way. With her unfading glow,
What may not youth and vigor know?

V

Yet dear as hope is, dearer still
Is Faith; faith in one's self; faith to fulfil
Whatever man has strength to will;
Faith to climb, but greater faith to stand
With patient, yea, with folded hand,
If need be, letting life itself translate
The hidden meaning of the order, 'Wait.'

VI

But if you find your day
Amid the thunders of the fray,
Even until the night is born,

And deeper night descend, without a star,
　　　Without a hint, a ray,
　　　A promise of the morn,
　While all your soul in anguish
　Feels and owns the battle's scar,
　　　Oh, faint not, nor languish,
　　　But press on, amid the throng
　　　Stalwart, brave, and strong ;
　　　Till others of your strength partake,
　　　　And you make
　　The echo that shall roll
　　Forever on from soul to soul;
　　The echo that shall witness be
　　Of your best claim to Immortality.

VII

And doubt not.　Life will yield its own to each.
　　　Let nothing slip beyond your reach ;
　　　　For in its wise economy
　　All things are good.　To use aright
　Is the true secret of the master's might ;
　　　　And he who with sincerity
　　Still follows well the light within
　　Shall make and shape the greater light

For which we wait. The grander day
      It is with you to usher in.
Its call is sounding even as we speak;
      Shall you its voice obey,
Or shall you craven prove and weak?
A land of promise is your own;
   But promise in itself alone
May be but subterfuge, and cloud the way.
         'T is action, action, the world needs;
They only live who mark the way with deeds.

VIII

With honest, earnest, manly deeds;
      Deeds that shall prophetic be
      Of all Love's vast immensity;
Deeds that stir to nobler aim,
      And still proclaim
    The value of life's creeds.
Nor let the soul in easeful sloth
Forget the meaning of true growth;
But upward, onward to the Mount, until you see
   The very height of God's Eternity,
Or show yourself transfigured, even as did He.
     Oh, tremble not;
     Nor let some spot

Upon the hour obscure your sun.   Keep the brave
    heart
    Of day, of night a part;
With all great thoughts of high emprise
Forever shining from your eyes.

IX

And here we pause.   Your gracious Mother speaks,
    Her heart the while o'erflowing in her eyes,
    As all in vain she seeks
            To quell the feeling that must rise
            With thought of you.
            We hear her say,
            You are my sons,
            My life has fed,
            My hand has led
            You to this day.
If you are worthy, mine the praise;
    And, alas! 't is also true
            If aught you do
To merit blame, or question raise
    Of honor, worth, or truth,
I too must suffer, and my name
        Be sullied by your shame.

But oh, turn with me to the page
   On which is found your heritage
And my imperishable fame.
   While this is ours, I have no fear;
   The guerdon of my toil has tribute clear.
Behold the names! See other wreaths than mine
Around the annals of their glory twine.
      On battle-field, in legislative hall,
        In pulpit, and in scholar's chair,
   Wherever duty with its trumpet-call
      Has sounded, they were there;
They rendered unto me the Purple that I wear.
    Turn now again your sight
       To what may seem a lesser light:
         For not in highest place
         Will you its beauty trace;
    Its softened ray reveals
    What praise too oft conceals;
      Oh, find; and consecrate anew
      That homage ever and forever due
To those who in the silence face
     Life's humble labors and its pain;
       Who ne'er complain,
   But with unconscious grace
The soul's true temples build; nor seek to enter in,

  Content to leave with Him
  Whether they fail or win
 The mystic meaning of the life within.
These, these enrich me with imperial power,
These are the jewels in my crest
That give to me a matchless and unquestioned dower.
 And all this priceless legacy is yours,
  With all that it secures.
Its greatness keep, make its light your own;
  Nor shall you stand alone,
' The gods are to each other not unknown.'

X

And now, with all high hope and expectation,
 Shall your song be one of exultation,
Filled with all the future holds,
 And all the present still controls?
  Or shall its notes in minor key
   Come back to me,
  Wailing some lost opportunity?
Among you there are those
 Of heroic mould;
But whatever you disclose,
 My love and thought your lives enfold,

My hopes, and all that your hope shares,
   My aspirations and my prayers,
      Must ever follow you,
      False to yourself or true,
Whether the path go downward, or lead to heights above,
You cannot go beyond the circle of my love.

And here my heart reminds me of the few
      Who came, and passed away
To the bright vision of the Longer Day.
      They went while yet the dew
Was fresh, and all life's flowers gave
      The fragrance that is ever new.
So much is theirs we may not hope to save,
   For us remain the tears,
   The shattered hopes and fears;
      The morn cut off too soon,
      For them, beyond our gloom,
      The fuller, grander noon,
The Spring time and the eternal bloom.

XI

For you on every hand
    Duty waits.
Woe to him who hesitates
    At her command;
Or fails, when she is near,
    To keep the watchful eye,
    Or dare deny
To her the listening ear;
She will teach you how to see
    The wants of our humanity;
To make less cheap the lives of men;
To raise your voice and use your pen
    For Freedom, Truth, and Right,
And keep them sacred in men's sight;
    To love the land we call our own;
    This land with every Good supplied;
This land for which our heroes died;
    To love her not alone
For the greatness she has shown,
    And the grandeur she has known,
    Through darkness and humility
    Your love must be
The pledge of brave sincerity.
Let martyr's faith be yours to give,
    Enforce and prove her right to live.

But listen closest when she tells
   Of that benignant and eternal law
From which your soul cannot withdraw;
   Whose majesty forever swells
      The righteous plea
      For true equality;
   Written on all life's histories,
   Hidden in all its mysteries,
      The one thing ever to endure,
      Holy, true, and pure;
That each is part of that great Plan
That knows the God Himself in man.

XII

   For God, for Country, and Humanity
      The cry is given, —
Forward, now, with your undinted shield
Forward, until day to night shall yield;
Forward, with the soldier's might;
Forward, with the scholar's light;
Forward, until Truth prevail,
      And no foes the Right assail!
Forward, until Freedom's won
For every race beneath the sun!

          Forward, until you
Have proved your manhood true.
Forward, until Wisdom's voice
Resounds in yours, and bids the world rejoice.
Forward, until all shall see
And feel your deep sincerity.
Forward; let the heights you climb
Point men to heights still more sublime.
Forward, till the earthly way
Fades in the glory of Eternal Day.

HYMN TO WISDOM

DAUGHTER of God! O Wisdom, hear!
    Thou who art never sought in vain,
We would within thy court appear
    And prove the good we strive to gain.
Eager we seek the holy place
Where we may see thee face to face;
Daughter of Him who made the light,
Increase in us the power of sight.

Mother of Peace! A tranquil heart
    Abides with those who know thee best;
And they to life a strength impart,
    In conflict to thyself attest.
Oh, hear us, and our prayer attend,
Let this, thy peace, on us descend;
Let tumult find in us thy calm,
Through conquest raise the victor's psalm.

Mother of Virtue! in whose voice
    Is found the song to life attuned,
Oh, help us early make that choice
    That saves the soul its deepest wound!
But if the evil should pursue,
Do thou, dear goddess, ill undo,

And lead, oh, lead to that fair hill
Where Truth, ascending, beckons still.

Great Truth! Thy sun, within whose rays
  Earth's evils quickly fade or die,
Whose golden flame creates the days
  From which all sin and folly fly;
Within his gleam let learning find
That in itself it may be blind,
Or useless, idle, vain, and weak,
Until through thee its sources speak.

Divine consoler! — yea, and more,
  True counsellor, unfailing friend,
Whom mortals know and then adore, —
  To faltering youth thy guidance lend.
And thou who art forever young,
Show us the halo o'er thee hung
When He who made thee smiled, and saw
The full perfection of His law.

Hail, holy light! We feel thy power
  Enshrining sun and star and earth,
As truly seen in smallest flower
  As when we learn of planets' birth;

Yet holiest art thou when we see
In man himself thy majesty;
Oh, shine out then in human deed,
And crown thyself in human need!

All bounteous one! do not withhold
   The light that thou alone canst give;
Through thine own searching make and mould
   And prove in us the right to live.
Come! Take possession of our souls,
Be the blest vision that controls!
If thus thou answer to our call,
Though owning nothing, we have all.

INVOCATORY ODE
(Written for the Inauguration of a College President)

O SPIRIT,
    Maker of the heart,
From whom alone our every good proceeds,
Draw near and be Thyself a part
Of this great hour. Show us our needs;
      If we Thy purpose see
      It must be, Lord, through Thee,
All else Thy glory to conceal,
But, oh, do Thou Thyself reveal!

We would be wise.
      Great Teacher, still bestow
      The gift to know
Where wisdom is. Brighter than ruby's glow
Is the fair jewel it is Thine to give
To those who in Thy presence live.
The path of understanding we shall see
Only as we walk with Thee.

We would be strong.
      Make right prevail,
      Whate'er assail;
Hold Michael's sword within our hand,
With strength to dare and to withstand.

   We know the day
   Is worth the fray,
That all this conquest may be ours,
If his courage sway our powers:
   Nor make the battle less;
   The soul must know its stress,
And through the struggle win release,
And gain at last the promised peace.

We would be true.
   This above all.
Author of truth! On Thee we call
To free all men from error's thrall.
   Without this we must bondmen be,
   Subject to basest slavery.
    Fill with the truth the soul,
    Make the moral nature whole!
O voice of God! sound full and strong,
Until our lives the strain prolong;
Till it is clear in all we do
That we unto ourselves are true.

So mould each man
On grandest plan,
  Wise, strong, and true,
  Thy crown and seal on all we do.

　　　　So let possession
　　　　Win progression,
　　　Until the highest is attained,
　　And the manhood Thou dost honor
　　Prove the manhood we have gained.
And thus, O Thou who canst make great,
Show us 't is *men* that make a state ;
Then shall the nation stand secure,
And all that is of worth endure.

WEDDING HYMN

O SUN,
From out whose gracious rays
Came forth the day of days
When my dear Love was born,
Shine out,
And with thy brightness pay
Due homage to her wedding day;
Bring gift, in golden gleam,
A prophecy of good in every beam;
Rejoice with so much of thyself that in her lives,
Which she with loving joy to others freely gives.

O Moon,
From out whose peaceful life,
A spirit came to guard her own from strife,
Shine out,
And with thy softest light
Make happy Peace to rule her wedding night;
Let all thy rays in silvery sheen,
Whisper of coming nights serene;
Rejoice with so much of thyself that in her lives,
Which she with loving joy to others freely gives.

O Stars,
    From out whose twinkling beams
    Came radiant gleams
    To dwell, and find within her soul an added glow,
    A sunnier warmth than ever stars do know,
    Catch from unsetting suns to-night
    A ruddier tint — a hint of Heavenly light;
        Reflect her eyes,
        And make new beauty in the skies;
Rejoice with so much of yourselves that in her lives,
Which she with loving joy to others freely gives.

O Flowers,
        Whose censers swinging slow,
    Exhaled rare fragrance fed with morning dew
    To touch the breath that first she drew,
    Lift loyally your heads, and gayly smile
    With joy, the while
        In rich perfume
        Her bridal blossoms bloom;
    Cull sweet perfection from her face,
    And then give back your borrowed grace;
Rejoice with so much of yourselves that in her lives,
Which she with loving joy to others freely gives.

O Music,
    Born upon celestial lyres,
    And thrilling 'mid angelic choirs,
        Come nearer earth to-day,
        Whisper in my lay;
    Repeat the melody you sent
    When to the world her voice you lent;
        Swell in the air that tells
        The echoes of the bells;
    Be like her lover's heart,
    Of her own a part;
Rejoice with so much of yourself that in her lives,
Which she with loving joy to others freely gives.

O Love,
    From out whose very heart she came,
    Born from thy glowing flame,
Look down,
    And in thy glorious way
    Crown thou her wedding day.
Oh, nearer come — make thou her bridal bed,
Close by her side all future pathways tread,
    Help her to see thy face
    In every clime and place;
Rejoice with so much of thyself that in her lives,
Which she with loving joy to others freely gives.

And ye,
    O favored ones and blest,
      Whose hearts have been her rest
        Since life began,
Ye listen now, and hear, with all Love's pain,
        Her marriage vow ;
     Giving, where most ye long to keep,
     Smiling, where most ye long to weep ;
       Repress your tears,
       Banish your fears ;
Rejoice with so much of yourselves that in her lives,
Which she with loving joy to others freely gives.

THE MESSAGE OF THE DEAD
(MEMORIAL DAY)

ONCE again through the soundless street
    Echoes the tread of marching feet,
And once again the spring-time waves
Perfumed grasses over its graves.

Once again the immortelles bloom
Over the soldier's honored tomb,
While we a soulful chorus raise
To those beyond our meed of praise,—

The Dead, who speak in mightier tone
Than any living lips have known,
Who through the silence still proclaim
Message grander than their fame.

Hear it, heed it, O thinking men,
Send it afar with voice and pen,
Or else these sons have died in vain,
And you their mighty conquest slain.

Oh, hearken to it here to-day,
Hear it, and on your altars pray
For stronger hand and wiser heart,
Its good to guard, its word impart.

'We died,' they say, 'that you should be,
The voice of nobler prophecy,
Advance the soul-illuming light
That puts the shade of caste to flight.

'We died, O men, that you might see
The freedom that alone makes free,
Finding the doom of race unrolled,
Unless its men are self-controlled.

'We died our fellow-men to save,
From every shackle of the slave,
Make plain the "inward liberty,"
That lives the true humanity.

'And born of this, time's fairest flower
Yields unto you its priceless dower,
Its boundless good in fragrance now
Asks from your heart one loyal vow.

'Crown it with love that shall appear
As is the sun at noon-day clear,
Then wreathe to-day the blue and gray
With bloom that fadeth not away.

' The bloom that sees not in the past,
In war's alarm or trumpet blast,
One gleam of that dark hour survive
That kept the reign of hate alive.

' Oh, let the mantle spun in blood,
And woven for a nation's good,
Cover the errors that were made,
Errors in sorest anguish paid.

' The reverence that holds us dear
Proves the divine is with you here;
Let living hearts its blessing feel,
Service for them its witness seal.

' Forget not those who did not die
With broken heart and stifled cry,
Who kept the home and hearth fire bright,
Through tears that made no rainbow light.

' True soldiers, though they bore no sword,
Nor blazoned page their names record,
Thorn-pierced and wounded, brave and calm,
Their country's solace and its balm.

'O noble woman, unto you
Is our exulting tribute due!
Thy strength the conflict only proves,
Thy courage high the night removes.

' No battle is like thine, nor scar,
Life's midnights but reveal thy star,
Thy faith sublime, that never dies,
And all thy suffering justifies.

'Others there are whose names once dear
Now sacred in your sight appear.
No longer young, but still " Our Boys,"
Bearing a youth no time destroys.

'"Our Boys!" God bless them! Make them yours
In all that reverent love secures:
Keep smooth the path for faltering feet,
And unto death their wishes meet.

'They walked with us, they shared our pain,
They bore the old flag back again,
Its tattered folds an emblem still
Of all that earth can best fulfil.

'True to its purpose still they served
And asked not what the past deserved,
They proved the nation's steadfast power
In brightest as in darkest hour.

'Old comrade with an empty sleeve,
Keep the brave heart; great souls believe
The grander labor has been yours,
Rebuilding temple that endures.

'But one great sword may not grow dim,
Peace hath her victories to win,
Each linked forever with the morn
Where sacred harmonies are born.

'Sword of the Spirit, do thy work!
Until no foes in ambush lurk;
Protect the power that guards and saves
The instinct, that no soul enslaves.

'Come, Love and Peace, make good your reign!
Let all this land be your domain!
Till North, and South, and East, and West
Make of your gifts our country's crest.

'" Our Country," hallowed be thy name!
And sacred before God thy fame!
Mother of Peoples yet to be,
Sun-crowned with Love's sublimity!

'No dead stone from the past is thine,
On which some buried self may shine,
No night entombing ruins vast,
Its shadow on the day to cast.

'Thou art the present, in an age
Replete with ripest heritage,
One signal triumph all thine own,
Each man a king, thy gift his throne.

' May God-like men this gift sustain,
Through lofty aim its rights retain,
Make statesmen of heroic mold,
Dauntless in truth, in wisdom bold.

'" Westward the course of empire lies."
Thou art the West, whose sun-lit skies
Lighten the world, and point the way
To glories of the grander day.

'Thy children kiss thy garment's hem,
And lo! a virtue falls on them.
This holy influence caught from thee
Transmutes to loftiest destiny.

'This destiny we shared and gave
Our all of earth its hope to save.
Resplendent Hope! by thee enthroned
Where nothing human is disowned.

'To thy great soil our dust is wed,
Fit symbol of the love you fed,
While with our own are mingled those
Who faced, and fought, and fell as foes.

'Brothers in death as well as life,
Brothers to-day beyond all strife,
Brothers in holiest peace allied,
Long may its fruit with thee abide.'

This is the message of the dead,
In solemn cadence sung and said.
Its mandate true and strong and great,
Let life, not death, perpetuate.

SALUTAMUS

SOLDIERS brave in days of old,
  Facing dangers manifold,
Looked unto their king to cry,
' Thee we do salute and die!'

Service for an earthly king
Other ending cannot bring;
Whatsoe'er thy record be,
Death is all it gives to thee.

Christian brave, where'er thy way,
Thine it is with joy to say,
' King, to whom my heart I give,
Thee I do salute and live!'

Service for the Heavenly King,
Love and life eternal bring;
He alone true life can give,
Him we may salute and live.

REDEEMING LOVE

I KNOW, I know that my Redeemer lives;
   This thought to life its highest glory gives;
But, O my Soul, how much of this is shared
With those for whom no portion is prepared?

He lives in self-surrender like His own;
Have I in truth such self-surrender shown?
Then truly is His own redemption shared
With those for whom no portion is prepared.

My Christ! My Lord! This, this I cannot do,
Unless Thou daily all my strength renew,
And grant to me to give as I have shared
The great redemption by Thyself prepared.

Then though my soul dwell in some secret place,
And Thou alone its earthly record trace,
Yet surely is its own redemption shared
With those for whom no portion is prepared.

PRAYER

A SABBATH peace is on the earth,
    A Sabbath quiet in the air;
Oh, let them touch my heart, dear Lord,
    And quicken it to thoughtful prayer.

To prayer that freely goes to thee
    With eager wish to know thy will,
Content to let the blessing wait,
    And all its own great law fulfil.

For well I know, thou God of Love,
    No soul finds Thee by word alone;
Oh, make my life itself a prayer,
    A constant pleading at Thy throne!

TRUST

I SEE not what the day may bring,
    I know not what the night may yield;
But one great thought my soul doth fill:
    God is my Light, my Hope, my Shield.

I may not walk where others lead,
    Some faiths I do not comprehend;
But this I know: that God is Love,
    And He will all my ways attend.

I may not keep one worldly gift,
    So much to me this life denies;
But with the Bread of Life He fills,
    My hungry soul he satisfies.

All earthly loves know change and loss,
    All earthly glories pass away;
But He supplies the life, the loves,
    That know no shadow of decay.

Let then the day bring what it will,
    And still the night its portion yield;
I walk serene, upheld by Him
    Who is my Life, my Light, my Shield.

COMMUNION

COME, Lord, and make Thy Presence known;
　　With larger light our lives endow;
Increase the love that can alone
　　A Sacramental feast allow.

This outward rite is poor indeed,
　　Unless the Christ is found within;
And He the Soul its portion feed,
　　Strengthen the heart, and cleanse from sin.

Awake, O Soul! behold Him near;
　　Through human eyes he pleadeth still;
In human form make Him appear,
　　Through human aid His hopes fulfil.

Reach out in this communion hour,
　　And touch with Him some brother's hand;
Bestow the food with Christ-like power,
　　And lo! beside you see Him stand.

WORTHY THY GOSPEL

WORTHY Thy Gospel, Lord,
    This is my prayer;
Worthy its thought of me,
    Its tender care.
Worthy its duties high,
    Waiting each day;
Worthy its Light divine,
    Pointing the way.

Worthy the peace it brings
    When tempests lower;
Worthy the home prepared,
    Won by its power.
Worthy the matchless love,
    Casting out fears;
Worthy its sorrows, too,
    Worthy its tears.

Lord, do I ask too much?
    Greater remains,
Thinking of Calvary's
    Agonized pains.
Worthy of this, O Christ,
    I cannot be,
Save as Thy boundless love
    Pleadeth for me.

HYMN FOR FOREFATHERS' DAY

GOD of the Pilgrim, in whose name
Our land was born through blood and flame,
Grant us to keep its altar fires
Fed with the torch of high desires.

Our fathers' God! we look to Thee
To give the Truth that made them free.
It was for this they lived and died;
Through this their deeds are glorified.

God of the nations! in whose sight
Men walk from darkness into light,
Give us the light our fathers saw,
Living and loving all Thy law.

Give us their singleness of heart,
Their courage unto us impart,
Their steadfast faith, unfaltering trust,
Their stern support of all that's just.

Their fearless following of the right,
Through days of threat and blinding night;
Their strength to kneel and praise and pray,
Though tempests swept athwart their way.

Through stress and storm they won for earth
The secret of a nation's birth;
The good they gave is ours to keep;
O God! let us its harvest reap.

DEDICATION HYMN

DRAW Thou near, O Christ, to-day;
Hear, oh, hear us, while we pray;
Grant thy blessing on this place,
Send new witness of Thy grace.

Here may worthy hope fulfilled
Prove the rock on which we build;
Its foundation all Thine own,
All Thy truth its corner-stone.

Here let sinners come and know
Healing touch for every woe;
Here let sacramental feast
Feed the greatest and the least.

Here let love forever reign,
Every heart its source attain;
Here let Bread of Life be given,
And the path made plain to Heaven.

Let each cross proclaim its joy,
Shade of selfishness destroy;
Show us how the life divine
In the human still may shine.

Thus shall His own Gospel speak,
Save the erring, shield the weak ;
And our lives, in true accord,
Find best service for our Lord.

EASTER HYMN

I DO not ask Thee, Lord, to show
    A recompense for labor done;
It is enough if I may know
    Some victory the hour has won.

But oh, I ask Thee to reveal
    The upward way that leads to Thee!
Whatever else Thy love conceal,
    This narrow path make plain to me.

And firmly keep my feet therein,
    My hand in Thine, whate'er befall;
One radiant hope without, within,
    Until the final summons call.

Then will an Easter morn be mine,
    And only death be found to die;
Love claiming life by power divine,
    And Christ himself forever nigh.

THANKSGIVING

FOR all the good that life supplies,
    For all thy sovereign will denies,
For mercies old and mercies new,
For skies o'ercast and skies all blue,
    I thank Thee, Lord.

For flowers that bloom along the way,
Yielding the beauty of their day,
For thorns that with this beauty come,
For all I get from shade and sun,
    I thank Thee, Lord.

For laughter, and not less for tears,
For disappointment, doubts, and fears,
For all that gives the strength to grow
In sympathy with others' woe,
    I thank Thee, Lord.

For enemies who bid me see
My weakness and infirmity,
For friends who wound as well as bless,
Increase life's joys, and share its stress,
    I thank Thee, Lord.

For Bethlehem, for Gethsemane,
For all the scenes of Calvary,
For so much of the Christ in me
As gives them perpetuity,
        I thank Thee, Lord.

For all save sin ; yea, even here
How wondrous does Thy love appear!
Without it should I ever know
The fulness of love's overflow?
        I thank Thee, Lord.

For those great souls who give to earth
The secret of immortal birth,
Who by their living light the way
To glories of eternal day,
        I thank Thee, Lord.

For aspirations and desires,
New born of pentecostal fires,
And saying still, 'Believe in Me
Through time and through eternity,'
        I thank Thee, Lord.

For all of Nature sun-suffused
With thought of Thee, and, rightly used,
Setting the soul forever free
To feel its own immensity,
    I thank Thee, Lord.

For that great law by which the heart
Discerns truth in the inward part,
And knows itself to Thee allied,
Thy love and wisdom verified,
    I thank Thee, Lord.

For all that gift supreme, divine,
By which men's deeds in splendor shine,
The gift through which our souls may see
He only lives who can thank Thee,
    I thank Thee, Lord.

For all we reach but cannot grasp,
For all the good we may not clasp,
For sleep at last for tired eyes,
And hopes beyond the day's sunrise,
    I thank Thee, Lord.

LIGHT AT EVENTIDE

IF shadows overcast my morn,
    And clouds its sunlight hide,
I only ask Thee, Lord, to send
    Thy light at eventide.

Though storms still hide my sun at noon,
    And darkness yet abide,
My soul submissive only pleads
    For light at eventide.

And while I plead, I know, O Christ,
    If I am near Thy side,
Life's storms will end in peace at last
    And light at eventide.

COMMUNION WITH CHRIST

I SOUGHT the star of Holy Night,
But sought it on that lofty height
    Where angel hosts were led,
Forgetful that its brightest rays
Are always on life's lowliest ways
    With truest radiance shed.

I found it not from earth afar,
The light of this all-sacred Star
    That leads, O Christ! to Thee;
I saw it shine in human eyes,
Made brighter by some sweet surprise
    Of loving sympathy.

The cup of water for Thy sake,
The wish to lighten hearts that ache,
    Reveal its light to me;
But most I feel its radiant power
When, in some silent, sacred hour,
    My heart communes with Thee.

CHILD'S HYMN

COME and join the music
    Of our happy band,
Ever marching onward
    To the Heavenly Land.

Come and join the banner
    Under which we go ;
Christ, the Lord, is Captain,
    And we fear no foe.

Duty is our watchword,
    Love our only shield ;
And to our Commander
    Only will we yield.

Kind He is and gracious,
    To His children true ;
And in every danger
    He will lead us through.

' Love ye one another,'
    His Divine command ;
Come and help us keep it,
    In our happy band.

LOVE AND WORK

'TIS not alone to feel Thy love,
    Though sweet that love may be;
I ask Thee, Lord, to grant as well
    True ways of serving Thee.

Teach me to feel my daily task,
    A blessing from Thy hand;
Make me to hear, each day I live,
    Thy gospel's firm command.

To work ere yet the night shall fall;
    To find in work reward;
To know that whatsoe'er I do
    Is done for Thee, O Lord.

And thus may love and work at last
    Win love and work for me,
Where all who live in love are found
    With gladness serving Thee.

MIZPAH

LOVE struggles with a thousand fears,
    Sees dangers yet unseen;
Unmindful of the promise sweet,
    The Lord will watch between.

Though all the space of earth divide,
    Oh, learn on Him to lean;
And hear His own voice say to thee,
    Thy Lord will watch between.

He knows what absence means to love,
    He knows the sorrow keen,
But gives Himself to those who trust,
    And He will watch between.

In safety bring His own at last,
    Where face to face is seen
The love that shelters and endures,
    Where nothing comes between.

THE CHRISTMAS GIFT

NOT what we get, but what we give,
    The Christmas blessing surely wins;
And most for him the Christ shall live
    Who now can say, ' I give my sins.'

GETHSEMANE

O AGONY for human words too deep!
The Christ is calling, and His own do sleep!
What earthly soul may not be now dismayed,
When he to sinners' hands is thus betrayed!

SCARS

SHE sought her dead on battlefield,
　　Her king of many wars;
And, finding him, she cried, ' 'T is he,
　　I know him by his scars.'

O record of a soldier's fate,
　　Whose light outshines the stars,
When she who loved him best can say,
　　' I know him by his scars ! '

'T is thus the Christian knows the King
　　Whose glory nothing mars,
Gazing at hands and feet and side,
　　He knows Him by His scars.

O happy we, if, serving Him
　　Till death the door unbars,
We merit then from lips Divine,
　　' I know thee by thy scars ! '

THERE IS A STAR

'The star, which they saw in the east, went before them.'

THERE is a star that lights my night,
    And whispers still of day,
Keeps hope awake within my breast,
    And lights my lonely way.

Without it, faith itself would fail,
    And love grow cold and chill;
It shines, and faith and hope and love
    My heart and being thrill.

Within its light I see the King,
    As did the men of old,
And all within its guiding ray,
    My eyes the Christ behold.

O blessed star that leads to Him!
    O holy, sacred light!
My soul looks up with reverent awe,
    And hails thee, Star of Night.

FUNERAL HYMN FOR A DISTINGUISHED CITIZEN

THE glory taken from our day,
   By grief transfixed, we scarce can pray;
Appear, O Lord, and by Thy word
Heal wounds of one unconquered sword.
    O Master, Master of the night,
    Come, bid our sorrow find Thy light.

This son of man was son of Thine;
We saw Thyself supremely shine
In all his mighty heart revealed,
While every deed for right appealed.
    O Master, Master of the night,
    Come, bid our sorrow feel Thy light.

The titles that he won and wore
Could only add and prove the more
The matchless worth of one great name;
Thou madest him man, this crowned his fame.
    O Master, Master of the night,
    Come, bid our sorrows know Thy light.

Here as above his grave we bow,
Thou wilt, O Lord, our tears allow;
Nor wonder that we scarce can pray,
Such glory gone from out our day.
    O Master, Master of the night,
    Come, bid our sorrows show Thy light.

THE BIRD IN THE BELFRY

A BIRD in the belfry
   Soars and sings, soars and sings,
  While the bell for the bridal
Rings and swings, rings and swings ;
    Cheerily now from his tiny throat
    His notes in a burst of rapture float,
    For the bird so high in the belfry tower
    Seems to feel the joy of the passing hour.

  The bird in the belfry
Soars and sings, soars and sings ;
  But the bell in the belfry
Tolls and swings, tolls and swings,
    And now I know this birdling gay
    Sings for himself the livelong day ;
    A hermit is he in the belfry tower,
    Tears or smiles have over him no power.

  O bird in the belfry !
Not like thee, not like thee,
  Does my heart in its music
Ask to be, ask to be ;
    Its notes must smile if others are glad ;
    Its notes must weep if others are sad ;
    And sooner far would I weep with the crowd,
    Than sing alone on the fairest cloud.

THE BARD'S EPITAPH
(A hundred years after)

ONE sleeps below whom men call dead;
A hundred years is what is said,
If here aright the record's read
    On this cold stone;
Yet, standing o'er this narrow bed,
    We hear men moan.

Though mourning still, we meet to-day
To wipe the old harsh word away;
While sunbeams pause, amid their play,
    To claim their share,
And laugh as though they too would say,
    'He is not there.'

He lives wherever daisies bloom,
Wherever hearts for Love have room,
Where scentless earth takes on perfume
    For beauty's sake,
And flowers fade not, nor consume
    The light they make.

Wherever man to man is kin,
And hate is felt the chiefest sin,

Where God Himself, above earth's din,
    Proves right to reign,
Because the lowliest He would win,
    And none disdain.

Where discord turns to melody,
And song to perfect harmony,
Where verse includes humanity,
    He leads us still,
And with the magic of his plea
    Makes strong our will.

And where majestic common sense
Its simple laws can best dispense,
And couple faith with hope, intense
    For human need,
We find him here without pretense,
    And learn his creed.

Beloved Bard! in song like thine
The world's immortal glories shine;
Oh, that we may like thee enshrine
    Our best pursuit,
And hold the powers that still entwine
    Great Wisdoms's root!

DEAD LOVE

TWO loves had I. Now both are dead,
    And both are marked by tombstones white.
The one stands in the churchyard near,
    The other hid from any mortal sight.

The name on one all men may read,
    And learn who lies beneath the stone;
The other name is written where
    No eyes can read it but my own.

On one I plant a living flower,
    And cherish it with loving hands;
I shun the single withered leaf
    That tells me where the other stands.

To that white tombstone on the hill
    In summer days I often go,
From this white stone that nearer lies
    I turn me with unuttered woe.

O God, I pray, if love must die,
    And make no more of life a part,
Let witness be where all can see,
    And not within a living heart.

RUSSIA

State

A MIGHTY figure chained to rock,
    A vulture feeding on its life;
The key that might the chain unlock
    Held by a fate that murders strife.

Church

The loaves and fishes, but no Christ;
    Husks fed to living, hungry souls;
Hearts longing, yet by lust enticed,
    Of flesh the idol it enfolds.

People

As one who lifts her hands by night,
    Nor dares to raise them in the day,
Knowing a woe the sun would blight,
    Yet stifled if by sun she pray.

SONGS WITHOUT WORDS

A MOTHER sings to her sleeping babe
    A lullaby soft and low;
But deep in her heart she keeps a song
    That words can never know.
        For speech is shallow, and silence deep;
        What hearts feel most they cannot speak;
        And the sweetest songs we sing below
        Are those that words can never know.

A lover brings to his waiting bride
    A message tender and true;
But the song that wakens love to life
    No language ever knew.
        For speech is shallow, and silence deep;
        What hearts feel most they cannot speak;
        And the noblest songs we sing below
        Are those that words can never know.

A maiden kneels at a sacred shrine,
    Seeking a blessing meet;
But the truest prayers that Heaven hears
    No human lips repeat.
        For speech is shallow, and silence deep;
        What hearts feel most they cannot speak;
        And the truest prayers we breathe below
        Are those that words can never know

THE BIRD AT MIDNIGHT

I

I HEARD a bird at midnight sing,
    Unmindful of the gloom;
His clear notes filled the darkened air,
    And brightened all my room.

        O happy bird! with love's own dower
            Thy gift my senses mark;
        And I would own, like thee, the power
            To sing when all is dark.

II

Forgotten was the midnight drear,
    The night no more seemed long;
For in my heart I caught and kept
    The echo of that song.

        O happy bird! with love's own dower
            Thy gift my senses mark;
        And I would own, like thee, the power
            To sing when all is dark.

III

And oh, dear bird, I learned from thee
  That song has truer ring,
If when the shades are dark and deep
  'T is given the strength to sing.

> O happy bird! with love's own dower
>   Thy gift my senses mark;
> And I would own, like thee, the power
>   To sing when all is dark.

CRADLE SONG

O SLEEP! with thy soft hand
    Touch thou my baby's brow;
With thy soft kiss, O Sleep,
    Seal thou his eyelids now;
Take him where quiet hours
    All peaceful blessings bring;
Show him thy fairest scenes,
    Thy sweetest murmurs sing,
O Sleep! thy murmurs sing
        To my king.

If Heaven should ask my child,
    Dread fear my heart would fill;
But, Sleep, I give to thee,
    Nor think, nor dream, of ill;
Yet with thy restful love,
    From Heaven I know thou art,
No other place could yield
    The good thou canst impart.
O Sleep! thy murmurs sing
        To my king.

Do thou while darkness reigns
    Lead him to realms of light;
Show him the land where day
    Is never lost in night;
Bring him from scenes like these
    Safe when the darkness flies,
And Heaven I too shall see
    Deep in his radiant eyes.
O Sleep! thy murmurs sing
    To my king.

EARTH'S REQUITAL

A WEARY woman heard a people's praise;
All she had longed for freely now they gave.
Alas! they knew not that her saddened gaze
Saw roses falling only in a grave.

LABOR'S GIFT

TO keep amid the storm the calm,
    To know in pain the safest peace,
Seek not in ease a fancied balm,
    Nor ask from toil unwise surcease.

SERENITY

O BLESSING found in God-like soul!
    At last I see how thou art won;
Thy owner asks from earth no dole,
    Nor leaves an honest task undone.

THE NEW YEAR

ONCE more my hands a jewel bear;
    No mark is on its surface fair,
But deep within its heart I see
A single word — Eternity.

THE POET'S GIFT

MEN toiled, and toiled, so long, so long,
    Searching for one great truth, 't was said;
A poet came, and in his song
    The truth was found — a world was fed.

MY BEST POEM
(To a publisher who asked for my favorite.)

YOU ask of mine the poem I love best,
    And promise it shall have the larger light;
Alas! alas! far, far beyond the rest
    I love the poem that I mean to write!

SONNETS

MAN AND NATURE

I

GREAT Nature keeps her final harmony;
   It speaks in distant sun, in simplest flower,
As though through all some spirit did embower
With light and love its own intensity,
Or guard, unchanged, some inner melody,
   Where life to life reveals a priceless dower,
   That, interblending, gives to earth the power
To make a perfect whole in unity.

In sympathy with this, the soul receives
Her share, and answers clearly joy for joy;
Alas! not so with man. The spirit grieves,
Finding how he his fellow man pursues;
How man for man can every trace destroy
Of the great link he should be last to lose.

II

War, rapine, murder, lust, oppression, pain,
   These and their thousand ills inclusive are
   In the foul lists that do so grimly mar,
Or leave upon God's work its darkest stain,

Forcing a living death without death's gain,
  The night of earth without its moon or star,
  The things that keep Hell near and Heaven afar, —
O God! how long, how long must these remain?

'Some soul of goodness in things evil lies,'
One said, who knew of earth the worst, the best;
Yet even his so all-revealing eyes,
Yea, even his all-pleading human prayer,
But deepens to our thought one bitter quest,
Nor lightens for our hearts one deep despair.

III

Another spoke with love-illumined sight;
  But all the burdened birthright of His soul
  Won Him at last a thorn-pierced aureole;
Yet from His far enfranchised gaze the light
Still streams, and with its deathless, potent might
  Pervades the darkness, that without would roll
  And in some quenchless horror steep the whole;
With denser fold injure and mar the Right.

Is God less God because these things are so;
Or shall He from the abysmal womb of Time
Bring forth some seed to work their overthrow?
The seed is in ourselves; if here it fail
To yield its fruitage, want its perfect prime,
The gates of Hell against us must prevail.

DAWN

I

ONCE more the miracle is wrought on high;
    Light breaks; the east a speechless glory
        wears;
    A bride resplendent comes, as one who bears
The symbol of a love that cannot die.
For her the emblazoned splendor of the sky
    Makes pale the stars; and peaceful night now
        dares
    Question her peace, as one who unawares
Discerning strength not theirs, ends breath with sigh.

And yet, O Dawn! perchance thou art to-night
A golden ending, not a bride to morn.
Whiche'er it be, thy unheard melody
Fills all the world; while to our upturned sight
The Unseen Hand that can thy light adorn
Guards well the sacred secret hid in thee.

II

And, gazing thus, I think of those who wait
    For thee with longing heart and weary brain;
    Of lonely watchers by the couch of pain;
Of those for whom thy glory comes too late;

Of some in prison cells, waiting their fate;
> Of some who look from clouded eyes, and strain
> To catch some meaning that may yet contain
A glimpse beyond, and all its hope translate.

And so through all thy beauty comes earth's moan,
Its restlessness, its long repressed desire,
The mournful witness of an undertone
That saddens hearts however they aspire;
O Thou who canst from night all shade divest,
Send Thou Thy Dawn to souls that are oppressed.

TO CYNTHIA

AS when at eve the moon in splendor shines
    Upon a cloud, and forms a halo there,
  Within its lambent and caressing air,
And thus in warmth its light incarnadines,
And when such vision all the soul inclines
    To pause, and whisper an impassioned prayer,
    As though it saw beyond the scene so fair,
The deeper glow that Seraphim enshrines, —

Thus, O my Moon, thy love falls on my heart,
And there creates the halo and the gleam,
The azure loveliness, the silent thought
That does to prayer such sacredness impart,
As from thyself I feel the placid beam
That is with holiness and peace enwrought.

TO THE OLD YEAR

I

SOON with the multitudes thou too shalt sleep;
    Would I dare hope no day of thine would rise,
In ghostly semblance come, without disguise,
To haunt the senses, and in anguish steep
The soul, that it some cruel past may reap;
    See the false seeming, fair to outward eyes;
    Hear the stilled moaning, that yet never dies,
But feeds to fulness thoughts for tears too deep.

Such hope is vain; then Death has one sting less;
For who can count the years in happiness
Secure in this, and in this woe alone,
That ever each must add unto life's moan?
If time to come keeps this in memory nigh,
Then God be kind, and let death mean — to die!

II

What poisoned chalice to my lips finds way,
    That thus I utter thoughts so dread with fear,
    The hope defy that is of all most dear,
Shut fast the door to all that bids men pray?

Thus make a sword of life to pierce the ray
    Of righteousness, thus stand in sad arrear
    With all that brings the wished-for succor near,
The balm destroy that can such wounds allay?

To barter thus with life is death indeed,
A living death that only demons feed;
Oh, rather let imagination bring
The shining glory and the choirs that sing!
Unless great faith, thus crowned, have perfect sway,
The soul is dead, and man but breathing clay

III

Up, then, O Soul! arise, and bring to earth
    The shining glory and the singing choir;
    Though it be legend framed of man's desire,
Yet is it witness of immortal birth;
Let gloomy doubt and fear give place to mirth,
    Let loyal hope the song of joy inspire,
    With angel musings touch anew the lyre,
And thine own vision Heaven itself engirth.

Thus, as the old year passes into night,
Look up to find your stars securely bright,

And in the new day see the sun appear
As full of splendor, and with beam as clear,
As though no darkness intervened to say
'Behold how night is still the tomb of day.'

WINTER

I

WINTER, with all thy glorious majesty,
    And partnership with Spring, whose trustful sleep
Thou guardest that she may thy vigil reap,
And prove the fulness of thy harmony,
Amid thy most tempestuous gales I see
    How like a sovereign thou canst hold and keep
    Not Spring alone, but Summer's promise deep,
And covered with a robe of purity.

'T is fitting season for thy birthday, Love;
It symbolizes all thy strength and power;
Yet is there in thy soul one light above
All that its patient wisdom can embower;
For here the Spring and Summer's fruitage meet,
And thus a triple song of praise repeat.

II

The Autumn with its splendor, it remains,
    Chanting its message of supreme uplift;
    Has it no portion in thy radiant gift,
Showing its beauty and its well-won gains?

Yes, yes, this too in glory lives and reigns
    Within thy heart, whose inner currents drift
    Where one great Heart doth all their meaning
        sift,
Rejoicing in the strength thy life attains.

From thence, beloved, with His glance divine
Resting upon the good thy days enshrine,
Even as it rests on Autumn at its height,
Illuming all things with enriching light,
This, this, in love thou dost on me bestow,
And prove His power in sovereign overflow.

EASTER

HAD I been with the two who walked that day
    As on the road to Emmaus He passed,
  Their thoughts bewildered, and while shades fell fast,
Their eyes yet holden to the star-lit way,
Should I, near home, have asked Him then to stay,
    And as He broke the bread discern at last
    The Christ, or, when aside all fear was cast,
Receive the Easter blessing as did they?

Oh, question not, faint heart, but find Him there;
The road is open and He walks it still;
Hears human love yet whisper all its plea,
Sends Holy Spirit when it breathes its prayer;
With Easter light will evening shadows fill,
And, while abiding, break His bread with thee.

EASTER MORNING IN THE MOUNTAINS

THROUGH what supernal gates of glory now
    I watch the coming of the day.   The Sun
  Can only crown with glory beauty won
Through ages upon ages, and endow
A majesty that bids the spirit bow,
    As though it saw all miracle outdone,
    The speechless revelation but begun
That doth to this brief hour such feast allow.

Gazing beyond this height, O Soul of mine,
Canst thou not see a grander vision shine?
For if to scenes like these, by way unknown,
Thou camest hither, and dost claim thine own,
Canst thou not trust always to find thy place
And e'en in death no desolation trace?

ST. ANDREW'S EVE

O COUNTRYMEN of Burns, who meet to-night
    To honor that great land that gave you birth,
    To pledge anew, 'mid toast and song and mirth,
The patron saint of Courage, Truth, and Right,
Rise as one man, and with your hearts alight
    Pledge ye one more among the great of earth;
    To fair Columbia's shores join Scottish firth,
Let Scottish hearts her newer annals cite.

Columbia, — yea, call her what you will,
She is the daughter of the nations still;
She gained a torch from your own mighty sires,
That lit and fed a thousand quenchless fires;
She asks you now to reillume their gift,
And thus the manhood of your day uplift.

TO G. H. E.

ONE season showeth ever life complete,
    The fulness of all loveliness and charm;
  Decay itself it seemeth to disarm,
As all things joyous in its throbbings meet;
Earth's fairest trophies lie about its feet,
    As though they were secure from all alarm,
    Or Heaven bent down to save from threatened harm,
Or spheric laws held Love safe from defeat.

To this so perfect hour I liken thee;
Thou dost repeat its richest melody,
Its warmth and beauty, all its strength and cheer,
Its deep serenity, its want of fear;
Yea, more is thine; in thee are crowned the whole
With the rich splendor of a radiant soul.

TO THE TREES ON MY LAWN
I

YE proofs of miracles, in beauty wrought
    By changing seasons as they come and go,
    What silent self revealings do ye show
Of a great glory coming all unsought!
Sun, moon, and stars upon ye shine; and fraught
    With splendor is the pageant that ye know;
    Storms visit ye; from ceaseless overflow
Of light and shade your mystery is caught.

And yet, ye witness of security,
Oh, tell me, can ye see and do ye hear
Something of that sublimer harmony
That lifts the life forever above fear?
Like Him who made, ye do so much reveal;
I seek the more to find what ye conceal.

II
Ah, useless, useless is the search, and vain;
    No sight in you an answering eye discerns;
    The longing look still the more surely learns
That ye have no response for joy or pain.

Oh, if ye had, should weary mortals gain
    A better light on all that hope affirms —
    A surer rest in all that faith concerns?
Or would the peace ye know with us remain?

Yet why, among your stately silences,
Such thoughts intrude? The rather let me find
Your gift to win from storm and sun and breeze
The strength to live, and keep the quiet mind;
Like you, serenely hold the upward gaze;
Like you, find heavenward growth crown all my days.

TO AN ANEMONE
(On the field of Chickamauga)

SWEET flower, tender, delicate and fair,
   From whence on this sad field came breath
      to thee,
And thy true whisper of earth's melody?
Can death to thee such fragrant beauty spare,
Or has thy life in death itself a share?
   If so, then death more manifest should be
   Of love's and sorrow's plighted constancy,
And love to hope a dearer message bear.

To quest like mine thou hast no word to say;
No answer to the hearts that ache and pray;
Yet, somehow, standing 'mid the dead this hour,
I hear from thee, O Spring-returning flower,
That howsoe'er men falter, fall, or weep,
What life has sown, life will forever reap.

EVENING ON LAKE MONONA

THE summer's affluent beauty crowns the night;
    Flowers and fragrance are on every side;
    The moon, arising as a joyous bride,
The water seeks and chastens with love's light;
While happy souls, enraptured with the sight,
    Find here no human sense its best denied;
    Entrancing melodies on soft airs glide,
And hearts responsive hold the vision bright.

If types we get in this fair world of ours,
Dim foretaste of the good that is to be,
Then surely does the charm this night embowers
Feed deep the longing for eternity:
For still the only pang its hours can send
Is the sad consciousness that it must end.

MOUNT DESERT

WITHIN her island home she sits enthroned,
    Imperial mistress of earth's fairest dower,
    All held and swayed with a resistless power;
No beauty that the world can give disowned,
The skies' entrancing splendor freely loaned
    To mountain, sea, and shore, each fleeting hour,
    While she its larger good can still embower,
And hear its grander melodies intoned.

Fair Empress, when within thy temple gates
Thy glory to my soul one thought translates;
And, gazing on thy scenes, God's ' Very good,'
Becomes the more completely understood;
I feel secure the hope He had in man,
Since He for man's possession thus could plan.

TO SHAKESPEARE'S MOTHER

WHAT strong, august appeal did thy son hear,
    When 'neath thy heart his own throbbed peacefully;
Or what proud vision could'st thou bid him see,
What flame-winged message carry to his ear?
Did God Himself to the unborn appear
    And whisper even then to him, through thee,
    Teaching thy heart thy child's sublimity,
While angels sang ' Earth's Poet and earth's Seer'?

Or was thy thought so full of coming joy
That, passion crowned, it held thee in its sway,
And poured the bliss of Heaven without alloy,
And led thee to the courts where angels pray,
Till there the King of kings looked down and smiled,
And thus placed His own seal upon thy child?

THE SERAPH'S SONG
At the birth of Shakespeare

O EARTH ! a son to thee is born, thine own,
Thine own forever, and forever dear;
To him shall heart of every man appear
As though he made it; yea, and all earth's moan,
The mournful sounding of its undertone,
    He shall repeat in living cadence clear,
    Unbar the gates of death, and without fear
Bid dead awake to make them better known;

See life in its supremest good and ill,
Know joy, and all the mystery that still
Unanswered spins its subtle web, and leaves
To other times the garnering of sheaves;
See the majestic glory of the soul,
And prove the crowning splendor of the whole.

HAMLET

SOMETHING, O Hamlet, of thy sad unrest
   Is found deep hidden in each human heart.
Heedful or heedless of some ghost's behest,
   Each soul must struggle on, alone, apart.
One faithful friend, Horatio-like, may yearn
   To walk beside, to comfort, to sustain.
Alas! alas! how early we discern
   No human power can help our doubt or pain.

Alone each walks, though all the world be near,
   The fawning Guildensterns on every hand;
Ophelias proving but an added fear;
   Alone we hear life's gravely stern command;
While still across one dark and soundless sea
   We hear the awesome voice, 'Remember me!'

ANTIGONE

WHAT lofty purpose held thee, holy maid,
    Thou signal witness of ennobling thought,
What mighty semblance of the Godhead wrought
Its way into thy heart, and on it laid
Such tribute to itself as few have paid?
    Can such self-sacrifice as thine be taught,
    Or does it still elude if it be sought,
Keeping itself in unseen garb arrayed?

Ah, faithful woman's heart! it is with thee
In every place this garb of light to wear,
Though only one has found the Poet rare
Who can interpret well its majesty.
Yet, thought sublime! that one thus glorified
Proves e'en the lowliest unto her allied.

DANTE

IF more, like thee, who into hell descend,
  Could bring its mighty meanings back to men,
  Proclaiming them with trumpet tone, and pen
Dipped in heart's blood, with echoing moans that
    rend
The lifeless air, show horrors that attend
  Sin's punishment, — oh, would some sunrise
    then
  Clear off the stagnant waters of life's fen?
To shaded way some surer signal lend?

Something that should withstay the wavering feet
Before they too the Charon passage meet,
And reach the soul that struggles to be freed,
Answering to the cry of human need?
Ah, Poet wise, if message like thine own
Be not enough, the heart is turned to stone.

THE BIRTHDAY OF BURNS

OF what avail are birthdays unto thee,
    O poet of the fadeless life and song!
Our earthly years can but thy youth prolong,
And death from death did only set thee free,
Exchanging earth bonds for God's liberty;
    Naught can Time steal, and in naught can he
        wrong,
    For Love and Time build only to make strong
The temple that resounds thy minstrelsy.

But if our lives should bring some truer tone
    Caught from the music of thy mighty heart,
That never could one human cry disown,
    That felt itself of every pulse a part,
If this were ours to offer year by year,
Eyes were less holden when The Christ is near.

WORDSWORTH

LIKE some great mountain peak wherefrom the day
Proclaims the sun, or where at mellow eve
He lingers dreamful, while our eyes perceive
An aureole, as though angels knelt to pray;
And restful as the quiet paths that stray
About the mountain's base, where flowers inweave
Their garments, and the summer breezes leave
Their sighs, when all earth's tumults die away.

Like all things lofty, always lowly wise,
Divine in simpleness, in reach sublime,
A reverence so great for Nature's wound
As owns its love, and thus earth's ill defies,
Or learns through ill Olympian heights to climb,
With heart attuned to every thought profound.

KEATS

BY sun-swept harmonies thy song was fed,
    O poet of the music-moving strain,
    Rising to ecstasy above life's pain,
And dwelling where all hymnic beauty led;
Hyperion to thee in his chariot sped;
    He robed thee in a garment without stain,
    Embroidered with the lilies of the plain,
And wove a crown of glory for thy head.

All this life gave thee. What did death secure?
A name in water writ, fair, clear, and pure,
Jewelled in loveliness, crystalled in tears,
Flashing its rainbow light across the years;
In hearts that live, a record and a place
The waters of the earth cannot efface.

OLIVER WENDELL HOLMES
November, 1894

NOT dead, not even sleeping is he now,
    Our honored bard, whom all our race reveres;
  In true and fuller glory he appears,
A crown of his own sunshine on his brow.
Transfigured is he on the Mount. We bow,
    Catching from there his smile. See what endears
    With clearer vision. Banish thence the fears;
Feel with new zest his charm each sense endow.

Then, coming back from this celestial height,
With chilling thought that earth has something lost,
We now recall, that air that's tinged with frost
Still makes the rosy flush of dawn more bright.
Dawn-like, O Master, was thy gift while here,
Dawn-like we keep it till the day appear.

WASHINGTON

IN all the land one object I behold;
    A lofty height with pure and spotless crest,
Always snow-crowned, yet too near heaven for cold,
    The sunlight ever finding there its rest;
Within its great heart mighty streams are born,
    And onward flow, through valleys hushed from strife,
Their touch awakening flowers that adorn
    Wide, fertile plains, where all things tell of life.

Toward it the weak may turn, and learn aright
    The strength and courage that can fearless be
In face of storm severe, by day, by night,
    Serene and strong 'mid all adversity.
O Good and Great! the mount is type of thee,
Who lived and taught the Freedom that makes free.

LINCOLN

IN all the heaven one object holds my gaze,
    Compelling witness of a reverent heart.
And ever, as I look, increased amaze
    That mighty soul does to my soul impart.
It bids me see in every clime and race
    The common bond that makes the world akin,
To find the fatherhood in every face;
    To feel the love that brotherhood should win.

With malice none — with charity for all,
    It led a nation in its darkest hour,
As though in silence it heard but the call
    Of Him who sent His own divinest power.
O Son of sons! all time to come will scan
Thy wondrous soul and cry, "Behold the Man!"

LUCIUS FAIRCHILD

HE gave us that which is not bought or sold,
    Nor seemed to know the measure of his gift,
Nor how its wondrous bounty could uplift,
And into nobler manhood make and mould;
Thus did his greatness and his heart enfold
    All human need, and still without unthrift
Expend; taking no thought to weigh or sift
All that in each less friendly eyes behold.

Earth gives her types of all that is to be
Eternal in its worth unto the soul;
In him we saw the perfect symmetry
That harmonizes and suggests the whole;
But in his friendship rare we felt the spring
Of every good that earth and time can bring.

HORACE HOWARD FURNESS
After hearing him read a drama of Shakespeare's

SOME seasons come to human life and thought
    That build 'great bases for eternity;'
    That leave an unimagined melody
Sounding from mountain tops before unsought;
And when such gift unto the soul is brought,
    Through well-appointed human ministry,
    Then has it new increase of sanctity,
And keeps itself henceforth in life enwrought.

'T is so it comes when Nature, one with Art,
Finds true interpreter in poet's heart;
All fair mid-summer glory now is theirs,
While each its royal wedding garment shares;
Thus is the Eucharistic feast supplied,
And the great Master's labor glorified.

ONE 'WHOSE PRICE IS ABOVE RUBIES'

AY, priceless above all that earth bestows,
Companion, mother, counsellor, and friend,
On whom the angels day by day descend,
To bring the blessing whose enchanting glow
Lights all the good thy loved ones share and know;
Through thee we learn how God to earth doth send
Those gifts that with His own great nature blend,
And how the earth-life gives them place to grow;

We see a deeper meaning in the line
'The Lord is with thee,' as His soul divine
Leads us with thee to many a sacred feast,
Where thine own heart discerns of want the least,
And thine own whisper wins from Eye benign
The glance that changes water into wine.

TO A MOTHER
Who wrote under her children's picture 'These are my Poems'

YEA, poems to immortal beauty born
    Are thine, O mother beautiful and fair,
    Verse written by God's hand, in witness rare,
Of all that may His deeper thought adorn,
To prove the freshness of celestial morn;
    They unto thee His whispered message bear
    In ways with which no other can compare,
Are never unto lover's heart outworn.

This is the poetry that never dies,
But to the heart undying song supplies,
That makes the barren place produce the rose,
And unto love its secrets best disclose,
Giving to human face the Father's light,
And to His praise our lesser strains unite.

TO A FRIEND
Who sent a vase of roses

TO what have I not likened thee, O friend?
   To the blest sunbeam that secures the day,
   To placid loveliness of moonlit ray,
To all that Nature and God's love doth send
To guard life's sacred portals, and defend
     The soul's best hope; to hour when angels pray,
   To tranquil lights that fiercest storms allay;
To those who on Christ's 'little ones' attend.

And now thy gracious gift adds one thing more
Unto my heart's already bounteous store;
Thy restful beauty fallen on the rose
Makes every flower a dearer life disclose;
Ah, the Eternal Soul breathes deep in thee,
And all things fair reflect thy ministry.

TO THE AUTHOR OF 'SONGS OF NIGHT AND DAY'

HOW does the poet aught of night reveal?
    Is it not ever day deep in his heart?
Has not some portion of its light a part
And place within his soul naught can conceal?
Yea, from the night itself does he not steal
    A beam as sure and strong as lightning dart
    That bids the deepest sign of darkness start,
The purest ray of vision own and feel?

Ay, noble poet of the Songs of Night,
The day is thine, it shines in every thought,
All luminous, and like a summer's light
When it with beauty of the morn is wrought;
Or if the night is touched by thee it glows,
The radiance of eternal starlight shows.

TO A BEAUTIFUL CHILD

ALL love's religion, with its light and quest,
    Should now be mine, to sing thy praises, dear;
For all that is of worth came with you here;
Great Nature gave her truest and her best,
Her own praise singing at thy sweet behest,
    Bestowing every good afar or near,
    Yea, yielding without shadow of a fear
All beauties born in her great-hearted breast.

If then my pen could catch one dimpling smile,
Keep but one glance of thy so-lustrous eyes,
Seize one stray gleam of gold from out thy hair,
And weave into its verse thyself the while,
The world would then read on in glad surprise,
And praise would then be mine beyond compare!

THE PROMISE

THE sunset falls upon the land to-night,
    With all its wonted splendor, joy, and peace,
    No whisper that the glow can ever cease
In one fair hope concealed within its light;
The stars appear, and on the heavens write
    An added promise, with the day's release;
    And thus the darkness can itself increase
The faith that lives behind all human sight.

Yet, standing near thy new-made grave, O friend,
    It is not from these scenes I gain in trust;
If this were all, my heart must still attend
    The sentence, 'Earth to earth and dust to dust';
But, thinking of thy soul, through all the space
I hear, ' Thy servants, Lord, shall see Thy face.'

TO THE TEACHER ON HIS BIRTHDAY.

LET other men count time by days, by years,
    To thee belongs another, grander way,
    And one that shall more fittingly obey
The high command of all that life reveres.
Count it by the memory that endears
    Thy labor; by the heart throbs that so sway
    Our pulses, as we meet round thee to-day,
And own a gratitude 'too deep for tears.'

We count it by the seed thy work has sown,
We mark it on that radiant vesture wrought
To bury ignorance, and seal its tomb;
We read it where great wisdom rears her throne,
And in the majesty of that fair thought
That makes the barren place know fadeless bloom.

THE EDUCATOR

THERE are those kings whom men in state still crown
With earthly trappings of great pomp and might;
The dazzling fashion of a day's delight,
Subject alike to unearned smile and frown;
And there are those who claim not earth's renown,
Yet wear it with an all unconscious right;
Yea, crowned and glorified, in all men's sight,
They bear aloft a torch no seas can drown.

For these, by sovereign gift from King of kings,
Know the full meaning of the Voice that said
'Let there be light;' are by its choral led,
And, climbing heights where its best mandate rings,
Bid those who follow see the vision blest,
Until within God's hand their own is pressed.

BACCALAUREATE SUNDAY

FAREWELL! your heart to mine conveys the thrill
   Of restless thought, of new untried desires;
   The sun itself has not more burning fires,
Or seeks the more a purpose to fulfil
Than ye, who with youth's strength and dauntless will,
   Look longingly toward noon; see distant spires
Answering to music of celestial choirs,
Your fair hope faithful to its promise still.

Oh, reverently go, as into vale
   Sacred to rising day! With rainbow light
Its storms illume! Touch firm and sure the sod
Of earth; yet towering heights beyond assail
   And win! Make darkness by your being bright,
And prove yourselves in partnership with God.

EMPEROR AND MARTYR

IN purple and fine linen, Cæsar stands;
    Imperial power in gesture, word, and tone,
    In beauty like a God upon a throne,
Though nothing Godlike breathes in his commands.
Before him one in prison garb, whose sands
    Are nearly run, now doomed to go alone
    To fearful death; and though he makes no moan,
His moaning followers weep in many lands.

The first knew all that earthly pomp can give,
The other suffered all that life bestows;
To whom belongs the truest right to live?
Which name with greater influence o'erflows?
Each called of God, — how did each meet His call,
The Emperor Nero, and the martyr Paul?

WASHINGTON'S BIRTHDAY

TIMES are there in our land when the great
    gift,
By the world's heroes striven for and won,
Seems by the lust of vandals quite undone;
When Liberty herself cannot uplift
The seething mass of fetid soils that drift,
    And make the darkness plain upon her sun;
    Thus fear and doubt our hope assail; we shun
Our faith, or cry 'Come, Lord, with vengeance
    swift!'

O Mighty Leader! then we think of thee,
Fearless in that dread hour that saw no light,
We hear thy sovran voice, with Saviour tone,
And now, such strength hath thy sublimity,
We see the cloud's true meaning from thy height,
And find thy presence still on Freedom's throne.

ARMENIA

ARISE, O brothers of the Christ, arise;
    Again within Gethsemane He calls,
    Again on sleeping ears His moaning falls,
Oh, woe to follow and not hear His cries!
His wounded form on earth's cold bosom lies,
    In agony that stoutest heart appalls;
    Yet those who own His name still stand in thralls,
While Pity, with her wounded pinion, flies.

O living dead! in ruthless murder slain,
Ye shall arise and in His glory reign;
But dare we pray that from your blood shall flow
Some fount to heal or lessen human woe,
Or hope that they who wrong you are the few
Of whom He says, 'They know not what they do'?

THE ARTIST

IS it to toil with cunning hand and brain
    To make a canvas live, a picture speak,
    The master's touch reveal, or, failing, seek
By stronger effort to change loss to gain?
Or is it still to labor to obtain
    Some dazzling prize, that, like a lofty peak,
    Sun-crowned, but tends to make the gazer meek,
By proving heights he cannot yet attain?

'T is well to struggle; noble to aspire;
Though art is long, and life too swiftly sped,
For longing souls with but one high desire
Are from divinest sources surely fed;
But he is artist, teacher, and high priest,
Who, in revealing self, supplies a feast.

THE FAITHFUL SERVANT

OH, say not 'dead' of him, the man of deeds,
   Who unto labor largest bounty gave,
  Nor sought this measure of his life to save;
Walking wherever sternest duty leads,
With strength that from her counsel still proceeds.
   Do gifts like these find only closing grave?
   That were to stifle all our hearts can crave,
To lessen what the world so sorely needs.

Yea, more, it were to wrong the Mighty Heart
Of which his own is still a throbbing part;
To dream that such a waste confounds His plan,
Though we its hidden purport may not scan;
But this we know; it was to such He said
'Well done!' and to His joyful pathways led.

A GOLDEN WEDDING

SOMETHING of Eden's golden hour remains
    Our earth to bless. 'T is found in golden
        days,
When beauty adds to light a softened haze,
Revealing all our universe contains
As though it were a bride, whose blushing gains
    A deeper charm because her blush betrays
    To Love love's secret, while her artless ways
Beguile his sense and win his sweetest strains.

But holy is this golden hour when found
In human lives made beautiful by years
Of faithful love, and two true hearts are bound
As one, with service each to each endears;
For such may golden bells of earth resound,
And Heaven's smile at last replace earth's tears.

LOVE'S YOUTH

I SAW two walking in a forest glade
   At set of sun; a man and woman, bent
   With age; the fading light a glory lent
To all things, and for them a halo made.
Behind them came two lovelier forms, arrayed
   In garb of long ago; a maiden sent
   Of God to walk beside a youth, prevent
The earth-soil, keep serene and undismayed.

The aged, turning, saw the vision, knew
It was themselves, fair shadows of the past;
Saw through old eyes life's chrism and its dew;
Felt the old charm that can its source outlast,
Then said: ' 'T is outward, it can only flee;
' Our youth is safe in Love's Eternity.'

LOVE'S POWER

LOVE seeks in myriad ways to prove the power
    Of love ; it searches earth and air and sky
    For one fair object that will typify
Its matchless and imperishable dower;
And though it fail love's glory to embower,
    Since naught that lives can with its essence vie,
    Yet is it sweet to let some tribute lie,
As lies the dewdrop on the breast of flower.

Beloved, like a star that crowns the night,
Dissolving in transparence all the gloom,
Serenely proving an unfailing light,
Whose mystic strength all shadows can illume,
Oh, this is like thy helpfulness to me !
If aught is worth, it has its birth in thee.

WHERE LOVE IS THERE IS HARMONY

FULL cadence falls not on the human ear;
    Some discord mingles ever with the strain;
    The melody we hoped we might attain
Eludes us, even when it seems most near;
The note of Hope ends in the sigh of Fear;
    The perfect is by imperfection slain;
    The vulgar hind can highest good arraign,
Till faith lies buried in an open bier.

All this I thought, until one day Love came,
And lighted all my path with gorgeous flame;
The discord now in melody is lost,
All fear unto the passing wind is tost;
He makes such music in my soul for me,
I own the fountain of life's harmony.

TO THE MADONNA

I

WHAT thoughts were in thy heart, O Maiden fair,
    When that full message from the angel came,
    That should bestow on thee earth's greatest name?
What strength and faith didst thy young soul upbear?
On what transfiguring height didst thou breathe air
    That steadied thee, facing thy matchless fame,
    Or, gazing into heaven with thy new claim,
Didst thou behold from earth some vision rare?

Ah! sweet it is to know thee, woman still,
One yielding simply to the Father's will,
Serenely walking ways of woe and strife,
Nor yet beholding all the hidden life,
But conscious whatsoever way is trod,
The son of man is also son of God.

II

All restful, too, that in His time and place,
    Thou shalt in peace all wished-for blessing share,
    His diadem of truest beauty wear,
And read the record years do not erase.

Not seeking what the Unseen Power shall trace,
   As thou for ministry of life hast care,
   Sublimely sure no failure can impair
The angel message, or its worth efface.

And when the hour at Cana comes to thee,
Refulgent in its star-crowned majesty,
So gentle is thy softly whispered prayer,
Thy Son alone can all its import bear,
Revealing unto Him the woman's soul
Christ-like in its compassionate control.

FORGIVENESS

TO eye of sense a vision unsurpassed,
    A beauty filling earth and sky and air;
    The glory of the summer everywhere,
Flood, forest, field, and flower, in splendor massed;
Within, a gift whose blessings must outlast
    All earthly scenes; a bond of love so rare
    It could alone make barren places fair,
Keep clear the skies though darkest hour o'ercast.

And yet in presence of all this to-day,
I feel and know an agony and pain
Akin to hell. 'T was here I wronged a soul.
Can all the beauty of the world unsay
The word that stings like scorpions now, or gain
From lips of dead the peace that maketh whole?

GOD'S FACE REFLECTED

NOT in the glory of awakening day,
    Nor in the splendors of the falling night,
  Nor any spark of Nature's glowing light
Gives me the proof of this eternal ray;
Nor always in the churchly ordered way,
    Alas! too oft concealed in needless fight
    O'er non-essentials; struggle for the right
Baffled and beaten, sickened by delay.

But ever is its radiance secure,
    The silent witness of undying love,
With harvest hour whose fruit is sound and sure,
    And gently leading to the hills above,
When, shining, it is found in human face
Doing its duty in appointed place.

THE SABBATH TYPE

THERE is a special gift of air and sun
    That sometimes rests upon a Sabbath morn,
As though it would the earthly path adorn,
Give deeper proof of all that man has won
From Heaven; as if some holiness begun
    Proclaimed a partnership with God new born,
    And placed a crown on Love without a thorn,
A robe of glory by His seraphs spun.

Beloved, to this hour I liken thee;
Thou art its fitting type; the emblem fair
Of all its worth to earth, its harmony,
Its hallowed peace, its rest, its voiceful prayer;
Yea, more is thine, for wheresoe'er thou art
This Sabbath beauty makes of life a part.

LINCOLN

'He had no poetry in him.'
Recent newspaper item.

HOW dull must be the heart that so believes
    Of thee, who kept unsoiled the Poet's heart,
Until to deeds thou didst its words impart,
Though with unconscious strength it naught perceives
Of all that it in silence thus receives,
    Yet sends it into life like lightning dart,
    Still bidding its divinest rhythm start
When it some nobler cause of Justice pleads.

Sublimely tuned, and answering chord for chord,
In that great melody that moves the earth
To all that is by lofty soul adored,
Proving best title to the larger birth.
Great Thinker! who from deepest music brought
The Poet's deed, the Man's immortal thought.

LIGHT
Written in a volume of Tennyson

WHEN God first spake, He said, 'Let there be light.'
But what is light? the eager question calls;
'T is everywhere, on every bloom it falls,
On rock, on tree, on bird with plumage bright,
On rainbow hues, on eyes that tell of night;
In jewel's flash, its radiance enthralls;
In sun, moon, stars, its mystery appalls;
In all the universe, how great its might!

And yet what is it, — filling boundless space,
This wondrous gift that from a voice proceeds,
Yet voiceless, soundless comes, and leaves such trace
Of splendor in its ceaseless, matchless deeds?

Ah, find the poet's soul, with heart aglow,
And then what is the light thou too shalt know.

ON THE OPENING OF A NEW LIBRARY

GREAT thought that in a lofty soul found place,
    And now finds voice in miracle of stone:
    Not through cathedral door to books alone
We enter here; for all that good can trace
On human hearts we come; and, keeping pace
    With high endeavor, struggle to atone
    For loss elsewhere; for surcease from the moan
Of restlessness; for peace that shall efface

All littleness, and lift us to the air
Of larger usefulness and victory won;
Above all else, we seek within thy ken
For that Great Spirit, luminous and rare,
That once again proclaims what can be done
By those who live to serve their fellow-men.

ON THE OPENING OF A MEMORIAL GUILD HALL

IN memory of one so young, so fair,
   Whose life held yet the beauty of the spring,
   Whose soul still knew the song that angels sing,
What have you here that can with this compare?
Can fluted column, arch, or ceiling rare,
   One touch of her sweet innocency bring
   And hold it now? Have you some seraph's wing
That can such gift celestial hope to bear?

Ah, no! it still must be with those who strive
To build within some type of her we miss,
With lofty purpose make these halls alive,
By lowly service still His garment kiss;
Keep love with sacrifice forever twined;
Thus here may her dear spirit be enshrined.

LOVE'S GIFT

BELOVED, thou hast led me to Love's height,
    And shown me all the worlds his heart
        controls,
The breathless wonder of His touch on souls,
The fresh Apocalypse that is His right;
The dawn that follows upon starless night
    To longing eyes no sight so blest unfolds,
    For thy gift in its very being holds
The prayer-sought land where God Himself is light.

Yet high above this gift I value this,
That thou hast been its bearer unto me,
The God-Light has the truer, firmer sway,
Imparts more fulness of unfailing bliss
In that within its rays I dwell with thee,
And share the greater splendor of its way.

www.ingramcontent.com/pod-product-compliance
Lightning Source LLC
Chambersburg PA
CBHW032148160426
43197CB00008B/817